Kierkegaard
the Christian

An Anthology of Quotations

Robert B. Scheidt

A little time and I have won.
Then all the strife at once is done.
Then I may rest in valleys sweet,
Continually with Jesus speak.

Inscription by his instruction on
Kierkegaard's tombstone
—Tr. by Ann R. Born

To the one who honored me by choosing to wear my name.

*[Some wear the medal to their honor
and others honor the medal by wearing it.]*
(#1329)

Contents

Preface 15

Introduction 17

I. GOD 25

    The Father .... 1 - 32
    Worship .... 33 - 46
    Seeking God .... 47 - 66
    Christ .... 67 - 97

II. MAN 40

    Human Nature—Good .... 98 - 114
    Human Nature—Bad .... 115 - 129
    Good and Evil .... 130 - 156
    Kierkegaard the Author .... 157 - 186
    The Individual .... 187 - 211
    The Individual and the Crowd .... 212 - 238

III. Man the Thinker 63

Truth .... 239 - 270
Reason .... 271 - 275
Life's Goal .... 276 - 284

IV. The Christian Life 71

Faith/Faithfulness .... 285 - 306
Work(s) .... 307 - 315
Christendom .... 316 - 400
Purity of Heart .... 401 - 409

V. The Christian Life on Trial 95

Temptation and Trial .... 410 - 419
Obedience .... 420 - 429
Sin .... 430 - 455
Suffering .... 456 - 487
Despair .... 488 - 501
Death .... 502 - 517
Dying to Self .... 518 - 530
Repentance .... 531 - 553
Forgiveness .... 554 - 563
Prayer .... 564 - 567
Pride .... 568 - 573

VI. The Christian Life of Faith 120

Passion .... 574 - 590
Choice/Decision/Will .... 591 - 619
Wisdom .... 620 - 625
Justice and Judgment .... 626 - 629
The Future .... 630 - 638
Hope .... 639 - 644
Doubt .... 645 - 649

VII. The Basis of the Christian Life **131**

Historical Evidence for Christianity .... 650 - 654
Salvation .... 655 - 665
Christian Commitment-the Leap .... 666 - 706
Denial .... 707 - 710

VIII. The Inner Life **141**

The Christian Life .... 711 - 744
The Imitation of Christ .... 745 - 765
Silence/Stillness .... 766 - 783
The Inner Self .... 784 - 806
Humility .... 807 - 816
Existence .... 817 - 838

IX. Aspects of Life **160**

Wealth .... 839 - 863
The Esthetic .... 864 - 878
The Ethical .... 879 - 897
The Religious .... 898 - 923
Health .... 924 - 926
Friendship .... 927 - 932

X. Family **173**

Romantic Love .... 933 - 949
Love .... 950 - 994
Marriage .... 995 -1016
Children .... 1017 - 1031
Women .... 1032 - 1040

XI. Society **188**

Time and Eternity .... 1041 - 1065

Academia .... 1066 - 1077
Clergy .... 1078 - 1106
Bible Scholarship .... 1107 - 1113
The Bible .... 1114 - 1127
Church .... 1128 - 1135
Secular Society .... 1136 - 1197
Newspapers and Journalism............................ 1198 - 1219
Deception .... 1220 - 1238
Language and Precise Expression .... 1239 - 1263

XII. MISCELLANEOUS QUOTATIONS **223**

Aphorisms and Observations .... 1264 - 1406
Anecdotes .... 1407 - 1461
Parables .... 1462 - 1506

The Theater, the Clown, the Fire 1462
The Jinni... 1463
Conqueror and Possessor 1464
The Cup 1465
Guidance 1466
Reflecting God's Likeness 1467
Abraham, the Religious Man 1468
The Traveler Headed to London 1469
The Rebellious Captain 1470
The Government Loan Office.................................. 1471
Man Looks, God Looks 1472
Fear of God/City and Country 1473
Seeing 1474
Stopping the Train 1475
The Customs Clerk 1476
Praying in Truth 1477
Travelling Through Cities 1478
About Face 1479
Abuse 1480
The Bad Word 1481

Reformation 1482
Love and the Swallow 1483
Individuality 1484
The Pious Hermit 1485
The Most Important Point 1486
The Author 1487
The Crowd and the Sermon 1488
The Physician's Task 1489
Living in Our House 1490
The Peasant and His New Stockings 1491
The Emperor's Son-in-Law 1492
The Invitation 1493
The King's Visit 1494
The Rich Man and His Team of Horses 1495
Quantity 1496
The Source of the Spring 1497
The Tame Geese 1498
Haste 1499
A King Who Visits Every Day 1500
Accustomed to Unfaithfulness 1501
Going to the Deer Park 1502
The Banknote 1503
The Defective Throne 1504
The Swimming Instructor 1505
It Will Be a Frightful Night 1506

Appendix I Key to Sources—Books
     in Alphabetical Order 267
Appendix II Books in Order of Publication 273
Appendix III Summary and Evaluation of Books 275
Index 283

Preface

To become acquainted with Kierkegaard's mind is sheer joy; and this makes reading him and trying to understand him well worth the effort. Still, his prodigious output necessitates some kind of selective culling. He wrote volumes of "stuff" in his diary and journals. Therefore, I purposed to arrange, within this book, Kierkegaard's thoughts in quotation form on a variety of topics—*all* from a Christian perspective. The passages on more secular, philosophical or now-obscure matters were purposely omitted.

I hope that this anthology of quotations will serve as a handy reference as well as an introduction to Kierkegaard's thought. The reader should find a "bite-sized Kierkegaard" much easier to ingest. Same food, just easier to swallow. I imagine that not the least of the benefits will be a good belly laugh at the wit of a genius.

As a matter of probity, I did not omit quotations with which I disagreed, and I could not (who could?) omit quotations which were witty or humorous. Only a few quotations from his dairy and journals, obtained from two additional sources, have been cited. They have been selected because they refer to his conversion, private Christian musings, or are particularly clever.

Kierkegaard wrote: "To write a book is the easiest of all things in our time, if, as is customary, one takes ten older works on the same subject and out of them puts together an eleventh on the same subject" (#160). It thereby becomes necessary to admit that this project has been anticipated by none other than "the man" himself. The difference is that not ten, but twenty-two, books have been used—the official, public oeuvre being completely represented.

First comes a brief introduction and the list of topics, followed by the quotations, arranged under these same topics. The list of quotations under each topic follows the chronological order in which Kierkegaard's works were published (and in the page order within each book). Each quotation ends with attribution, given in parenthesis in abbreviated form—book and page number. The first appendix contains a key to the abbreviations. The second appendix lists Kierkegaard's works in chronological order of publication. Appendix three is a listing of the books with a brief summary of their content—once again viewed from a Christian perspective. All but two of the works come from the Princeton series translating Kierkegaard's works, supervised by Howard V. and Edna H. Hong assisted by a revolving International Advisory Board.

Introduction

Kierkegaard is difficult to read but meaningful when understood. He writes from another era, another culture, another perspective, and in another language; but his insights into life are by no means provincial or dated. His observations are astute, timeless, pertinent and overwhelmingly Christian. Truth is truth, and truth is timeless. Human nature has not changed; neither has secular culture nor the Christian church. Kierkegaard's critique of "Christendom" is just as trenchant today in our society as it was then in his. And it is strikingly more original! His writings yield well to memorable aphorism and quotation. Indeed, quotations are the easiest way to get to know the mind of Kierkegaard.

Søren Aabye Kierkegaard (Churchyard? Graveyard?), the youngest of seven children, was born into the family of a successful Danish lower-class entrepreneur. The father and the home life were both pious and melancholic. His father was deeply influenced by the Moravians as well as by his friendship with the titular head of the official Danish church, Bishop Mynster, who often visited during Søren's childhood. The adult Kierkegaard deeply distrusted the bishop's cultured urbanity, and in turn the bishop disliked him. Because of the Bishop's friendship with his father, Kierkegaard did not publicly criticize Bishop Mynster while he was still living.

Kierkegaard's father profoundly influenced him. However two admissions by his father shook their relationship. One or the other (or both?) were referred to by Kierkegaard as an "earthquake" in his life. Kierkegaard's mother, Ane Sørensdatter Lund, had worked in the house as a maid during the time of his father's marriage to his first wife who died barren. Kierkegaard's father confessed to him that he had had a sexual relationship with his mother before the death of his first wife. The other confession was that the father had "cursed God." Kierkegaard apparently feared that the sins of the father would be visited on the children, and the untimely death of every sister and one brother worked only to confirm his foreboding.

Kierkegaard lived from 1813 to 1855—not a very long life by today's standards. Nevertheless he outlived every sister and one of his brothers who died of tuberculosis after emigrating to America. Several of the family died at age 33, and Kierkegaard himself expected to die at that age. The brother who outlived him suffered mental illness in his old age.

Besides a melancholic disposition, Kierkegaard inherited from his father a fortune of 33,954 rixdalers ($400,000 in current U.S. dollars). He had probably spent all of it by the time of his death because, for the most part, he self-published his own writings, and they were not successful, except for his first and only popular book, *Either/Or*. He seldom traveled outside of his native country, indeed hardly outside of Copenhagen, except for three visits to Berlin.

During his University days Kierkegaard was somewhat of a wit and a dandy. He was popular with other students even though always a conservative, and his brilliant repartee in public debates and writings impressed students and teachers alike. He loved Mozart's music—especially the opera, Don Giovanni. He cultivated his love for the fine arts, especially music and theater, to the degree that he was able to write well-received critiques of the contemporary artistic scene. At the same time he was a typical student. He probably had a sexual "fling" or two (he may have contracted a sexually transmitted disease), and he accumulated debts, one of which, $12,000, his father paid on his behalf.

Four events influenced the course of Kierkegaard's career. In 1837 Kierkegaard met and fell in love with Regine Olsen. Even though at that time he was 24 and she was 15, he pursued and won her affection. He proposed to her in 1841 and was accepted. Almost immediately he regretted this action. In his diary he said of the relationship: "I was an eternity too old for her." He was also fearful that he would make this lighthearted girl unhappy by his melancholy temperament. Because at that time breaking an engagement was a scandalous affair and he did not wish to hurt his fiancée's reputation, Kierkegaard devised a scheme so as to appear that she had broken off the engagement. For several months he made a noisy nuisance of himself in public, by every means possible showing himself and his conduct to be worthy of her rejection. This event, falling in love and almost immediately turning from love, was seminal in Kierkegaard's career. It was as if he sublimated this failed relationship into the energy of writing. His insights into his own psychology and the psychology of romance became the subject of several passages in his subsequent writings (e.g. The Seducer's Diary section of *Either/Or*).

The second impactful event was his personal conversion. On May 9, 1838, he recorded the experience in his diary as follows: ". . . Indescribable joy that is kindled in us just as inexplicably as the apostle's unmotivated exclamation: 'Rejoice, and again I say, Rejoice.'—Not a joy over this or that, but a full-bodied shout of the soul 'with tongue and mouth, and from the bottom of the heart; I rejoice in my joy, of, with, at, for, through, and with my joy'—a heavenly refrain which suddenly interrupts our other songs, a joy which like a breath of air cools and refreshes, a puff from the trade winds which blow across the plains of Mamre to the eternal mansions" (*Papers and Journals*). His life took a dramatic turn subsequent to this experience. He became reconciled with his father, he ended his profligate ways, and he became serious in his University studies.

The third career-influencing event was his conflict with the Danish press beginning in 1846. The controversy seems to have been provoked by Kierkegaard himself in reaction to a superficial review of his book, *Stages on Life's Way*, by P.L. Møller. The revue appeared in a popular tabloid-like newspaper called The Corsair. Kierkegaard had become increasingly disenchanted with the superficiality of Danish culture, and especially that of the press. His public response to the careless revue and his scathing criticism of the irresponsible and shallow writing in public newspapers struck a nerve. The ensuing controversy, *The Corsair Affair*, filled the daily papers with charges and counter-charges much to the amusement of the reading public who, as observers, enjoyed the mayhem. All the advantages went to the press because they always had the final word. They personally attacked and caricaturized Kierkegaard's physical appearance and dress in such a way that he became an object of ridicule to the public. He had to give up his daily walks in Copenhagen, and he lost several friendships in the aftermath. This seems to have deeply wounded Kierkegaard even though he maintained that he was not personally affected. The positive result of this controversy was that Kierkegaard vigorously resumed his writing career instead of pursuing his plans to retire into a quiet country pastorate.

The fourth event was his public controversy with the Danish State church. When Bishop Mynster died in 1854, he was represented as "a witness to the truth" in a eulogy by the new bishop, Martensen, who succeeded him. This was too much for Kierkegaard. He regarded Mynster's career as more worldly than as a witness to the truth (of Christianity). He had refrained from public criticism of Bishop Mynster out of reverence for the memory of his father, but now the gates came open. Kierkegaard also tried to engage the new bishop, Martensen, in public debate, but Martensen defended himself only once and then chose to ignore the whole controversy. Kierkegaard opposed Martensen for his Hegelian philosophy and his Hegelian distortions of Christianity. Kierkegaard's incisive criticisms of Danish State Christianity are classic. They will always be relevant to any controversy between the established church with its, perhaps, lax and easy viewpoint in comfortable compliance with secular culture, and the more active and passionate church with its desire for purity and New Testament Christianity.

Kierkegaard did not live much longer after this controversy—he died in 1855. His authorship extended over the years 1843–1855 with several of his works being published posthumously. A lifelong opposition to the philosophy of Hegel characterizes Kierkegaard's writings. This opposition is captured in the title of his most popular work, *Either/Or*. Decisive choice and the necessity of rejection or "dying-to" alternative ways is expressed in opposition to the Hegelian dialectic of *Both/And*.

Kierkegaard paid little attention to current events and politics. The disastrous (for Denmark) Danish-German war of 1848–1850 and the subsequent liberal re-constitution of Denmark were matters of no importance to him. His concern was with the inner man, existential or personal choice, and the soul and its relationship to God.

Kierkegaard's writings are wordy (prolix). This was not just the opinion of his contemporaries; it was even acknowledged by Kierkegaard himself. How much more today! Reading him can be difficult until one gets used to his modes of expression. It would be easy just to give up. At times he is obscure—this may reflect the limitations of the reader rather than the author or his topic. No doubt one would better understand him if one were contemporary or spoke Danish. Nevertheless the translations in the Princeton series used here seem quite accurate, and they winsomely convey his mind. Kierkegaard's sentences ramble maddenly on and on, and his eccentric punctuation barely imposes order. His punctuation has been preserved in the quotations, as it has in the translations.

Kierkegaard is considered to be the first Existentialist—the first to write tellingly of the inner person and the subjective psychology of personal commitment. The whole Existentialist movement, including thinkers like Nietzsche, Jaspers, Heidegger, Sartre, Camus, etc., begins with him. Kierkegaard is also hailed as the precursor psychoanalyst. His descriptions of anxiety, despair, freedom, avoidance (repression) of unwelcome truth by protective psychological devices such as lifestyles of triviality or diversion, etc., is considered to be classic pre-Freudian analysis. If one interprets Kierkegaard only in terms of those who succeeded him in these movements, one will miss the defining mark of his authorship as he himself understood it. He wrote as a Christian.

Kierkegaard is referred to as the "Melancholy Dane," but he had a poignant and ironic sense of humor. If anything, he was a humble man who viewed himself as absurd rather than pathetic.

His writing is free of self-pity—at least until the bitter controversies with the press and their attacks on his person that made him an object of ridicule. Kierkegaard does seem to be someone with whom it would be difficult to get along if one disagreed with him. He could be blunt to the point of rudeness, and his irony bordered on sarcasm. He seemed to be spoiling for a fight during the controversies between him and the official Danish-Lutheran church. And he, himself, provoked the dispute with the news media (newspapers) of his day. Our modern view of him as physically misshapen, eccentric in dress, and melancholic in disposition is no doubt colored by the *ad hominem* attacks of his enemies in his contemporary Danish society. He seemed to take himself (not his task) lightly. Even at the end of his life Kierkegaard retained his sense of humor. When, at a public gathering shortly (days) before his death, he unaccountably slumped off a couch and onto the floor, he winked and remarked to his friends: "Oh, leave it. Let the maid sweep it up in the morning." There was never a diagnosis to explain his death.

Kierkegaard is largely misunderstood. Many Christians mistakenly think him too subjective. His term, "leap of faith," has become a pejorative term for many. It is felt (surely by those who have not read much of him) to be without objective (Biblical) criteria. To the contrary, Kierkegaard's Bible interpretations are refreshingly original, but never unorthodox. In addition many Christians think him too difficult or obscure. (Modern Christianity is not distinguished by its love of serious thinking.) Contemporary secular opinion assumes that Kierkegaard's ideas are at best naïve, or at worst arcane and gloomy. The answer to such prejudice is, "Come and see!"

The danger of citing quotations isolated from their context is the danger of misrepresentation. However, in the case of Kierkegaard, if we keep the quotations in their overriding Christian context, we have the imprimatur of the author himself.

Kierkegaard wrote of his authorship: "The essentially Christian is the category for my whole work as an author regarded as a totality" (#170). The best outcome from reading this collection would be that the reader would personally (existentially?) take up his books, see the quotations in context, and follow his reasoning at first hand.

Topics (Numbered Quotations with References)

I. GOD

God the Father

1. Thus a human being is great and at his highest when he corresponds to God by being nothing at all himself. (EUD-311)

2. It by no means follows, however, that a person's life becomes easy because he learns to know God . . . (EUD-324)

3. Did not the seers in Egypt perform almost as great signs as Moses? Suppose that they had performed greater signs; what would follow from that? Nothing, absolutely nothing with regard to the God-relationship. (TDIO-25)

4.   If a person does not encounter God in the resolution, if he has never made a resolution in which he had a transaction with God, he might just as well have never lived. (SOLW-110)

5.   God created man in his image, and in return man creates God in his, declares Lichtenberg, and it is true that the kind of person one is personally has an essential influence on one's conception of God. (SOLW-229)

6.   . . . For her God is very much like what one pictures as a kind elderly uncle who for a sweet word does everything the child wants, just as the child wants it. (SOLW-236)

7.   . . . The person who wants to come closer to God by disdaining what is simple, distances God in his exclusiveness . . . (SOLW-260)

8.   Although I have the most inspired conception of God's love, I also have the conception that he is not an old fussbudget who sits in heaven and humors us, but that in time and temporality one must be prepared to suffer everything. (SOLW-374)

9.   . . . Implicit in the concept of the fear of God is the idea that one is to fear him; and if it is dangerous for a person's soul to make God into a despot, then it is also dangerous for his piety to speculate God into a subordinate servant . . . (SOLW-378)

10.   To relate oneself existentially with pathos to an eternal happiness is never a matter of occasionally making a huge effort but is constancy in the relation, the con-

stancy with which it is joined together with everything. (CUP-535)

11.   Father in heaven! What is a human being without you! What is everything he knows, even though it were enormously vast and varied, but a disjointed snippet if he does not know you . . . (UDVS-7)

12.   . . . The task is to repent and regret. . . . To be abandoned by God, that indeed means to be without a task. (UDVS-280)

13.   The fundamental relation between God and a human being is that a human being is a sinner and God is the Holy One. (UDVS-285)

14.   . . . To die with a witticism on one's lips, that is a proud victory, that is paganism's triumph; and it is also the ultimate in human relationships. . . . An apostle, however, leaves out everything else . . . has his sights on God alone. (UDVS-336)

15.   Ultimately, love for God is the decisive factor; from this originates love for the neighbor—but paganism had no inkling of this. It left out God, made erotic love and friendship into love and abhorred self-love. (WOL-57)

16.   . . . Only the Christian knows that God's will is grace . . . (CD-65)

17.   The greatest distance, greater than from the most distant star to the earth, greater than any human skill can measure, is the distance from God's grace to God's wrath . . . (CD-68)

18.   The simple and humble way is to love God because one needs him. . . . It seems very elevated to love God because he is so perfect; it seems very selfish to love God because one needs him—yet the latter is the only way in which a person can truly love God . . . (CD-188)

19.   The person who most profoundly recognizes his need of God loves him most truly. You are not to presume to love God for God's sake. (CD-188)

20.   In the divine sense, not to love God is a human being's crucial wretchedness . . . (CD-195)

21.   Imagine two people, both of whom lost everything, but the one also lost faith in God's love—what is the difference between these two? Shall we in a wretched way say that the difference is that the one is still somewhat better off than the other? No, let us speak the truth, the difference is: the one really did lose everything; the other really lost nothing at all, since he indeed retained the highest good. (CD-199)

22.   There is not much use in speaking of God as the teacher and then have the instruction be only a purely human improvement program. (CD-386)

23.   If the difference is infinite between God, who is in heaven, and you, who are on earth, the difference between the Holy One and the sinner is infinitely greater. (WA-123)

24.   Indeed, just because God in the most eminent sense is personality, sheer personality, for that very reason what is official is infinitely more repugnant to him than it is

for a woman to discover that a proposal is made to her according to—a book of formulas. (M-173)

25. . . . God is indeed a human being's most appalling enemy, your mortal enemy. Indeed, he wants you to die, to die to the world. . . . The people who do not become involved at all with God enjoy—appalling irony!—the benefit that God does not torment them in this life. . . . But he is your mortal enemy; he, love, he out of love wants to be loved by you, and this means that you must die, die to the world; otherwise you cannot love him. (M-177)

26. But everything moves you, and in infinite love. Even what we human beings call a trifle and unmoved pass by, the sparrow's need, that moves you; what we so often scarcely pay attention to, a human sigh, that moves you, Infinite Love. But nothing changes you, you Changeless One! (M-268)

27. I learned from him what fatherly love is, and through this I gained a conception of divine fatherly love, the one single unshakable thing in life, the true Archimedean point. (M-383)

28. It is an extraordinary benefaction that you came into existence, it is a nice world you came into, and God is a nice fellow; just stay with him, he very likely will not fulfill all your wishes, but he certainly does help. A downright falsehood. (M-252)

29. My father died—I got another father in his stead: God in Heaven—and then I found out that, essentially, my first father had been my stepfather and only unessentially my first father. (D-33)

30.   . . . Wherever God is present progress will be recognizable by mounting demands, by the cause becoming harder. (D-171)

31.   The birds on the branches, the lilies in the field, the deer in the forest, the fishes in the sea, countless hosts of happy men exultantly proclaim: God is love. But beneath all these sopranos, supporting them as it were as the bass part does, is audible the *de profundis* which issues from the sacrificed one: *God is love. Journals* (KA-xxvi)

32.   God created out of nothing—wonderful you say: yes to be sure, but he does what is still more wonderful: he makes saints out of sinners. *Journal* Jul 7, 1838 (KA-10)

Worship

33.   . . . Because one demonstrates his (the King) presence by the expression of submissive-ness . . . one also demonstrates the existence of God by worship . . . (CUP-545)

34.   Worship is again the expression of wonder, and the range of worship is just as loathsome as it is ludicrous, just as erring as it is childish. If the seeker is assumed to be able to do everything to find what is sought, the enchantment is gone, the wonder forgotten; there is nothing to wonder over. (TDIO-19)

35.   And so it is with this wonder—it changes the seeker; and so it is with this change—it seeks to become some-

thing else, indeed, become the very opposite: to seek means that the seeker himself is changed. He is not to look for the place where the object of his seeking is, because it is right with him; he is not to look for the place where God is, he is not to strive to get there, because God is right there with him, very near, everywhere near, at every moment everywhere present, but the seeker must be changed so that he himself can become the place where God in truth is. (TDIO-23)

36.   Even if God's name is mentioned first and last, one still is not speaking with God if the conception [category] in which the worshiper expresses his thanks is not of God but of happiness, fate, the great prize, and the like or of an enigmatic power, whose intervention prompts one to be amazed—and to idolize. (TDIO-64)

37.   . . . The reward of the good person is to dare (to be allowed) to worship in truth. (UDVS-35)

38.   . . . A human being can praise God only by obedience, can praise him best by perfect obedience. (CD-85)

39.   Then, instead of becoming self-important by *demonstrating* that there is a God, humbly to demonstrate that you *believe* that there is a God, to demonstrate it by joyous and unconditional obedience—this is the hymn of praise. (CD-86)

40.   . . . Worship's only desire is that God will become stronger and stronger . . . (CD-132)

41.   Think how impoverished a person would be if he could live through life, proud and self-satisfied, without ever

having admired anything. But how horrible if a person could live through his life without ever having wondered over God, without ever, out of wonder over God, having lost himself in worship! (CD-132)

42.   . . . A Christian's life is a divine service every day: . . . The task is to remain at the Communion table when you leave the Communion table. (CD-274)

43.   A Christian's life is divine worship every day . . . (CD-393)

44.   True worship quite simply consists in doing God's will. But that kind of worship was never to people's liking. What occupies people in every age . . . is to arrange another kind of worship that consists of doing their own will, but in such a way that God's name, calling upon God, is connected with it, whereby people think themselves protected against being ungodly—alas, although precisely this is the most definite kind of ungodliness. (M-245)

45.   If two people are eating nuts together, and the one likes only the shell, the other only the kernel, they must be said to be well matched. In the same way God and the world also match each other. What the world rejects, throws away, scorns—the sacrificed ones, the kernels— God places an infinite price precisely on that, gathers it more zealously than the world gathers what it loves most passionately. (M-222)

46.   . . . Every higher conception of life (for example, even the best in paganism, not to speak of Christianity) sees the issue in this way; that the task for a human being is

to strive to be in relationship with the deity . . . (M-318)

Seeking God

47.   How well we know that the seeker does not always need to wander out into the world, because the more holy that is which he seeks, the closer it is to him, and if he seeks you, O God, you are closest of all to him! (TDIO-9)

48.   . . . How, then, does the sinner dare to seek you, you righteous God! . . . He seeks you in the confession of sins. (TDIO-9)

49.   Or was it not fearful, my listener, that what was sought was so close to you, that you did not seek but God sought you? (TDIO-22)

50.   If what is sought is assumed to be given, seeking means that the seeker himself is changed and becomes the place where what is sought can be present in truth. (TDIO-27)

51.   The more profound the sorrow is, the more a person feels himself as a nothing, as less than nothing, and this happens simply because the sorrower is the seeker who is beginning to become aware of God. (TDIO-29)

52.   And there is indeed a place for this [seeking to be alone with God], my listener, and you know where; and there is indeed an opportunity, my listener, and you know

how; and there is indeed a moment, and it is called: this very day. (TDIO-36)

53.   As a *human being* he was created in *God's image*, but as a *Christian* he has God as the *prototype*. . . . A prototype is certainly a summons, but what a blessing! (CD-41)

54.   Presumptuousness pertains essentially to a person's relationship to God; and this is why it is inconsequential whether a person presumes in the least or in the greatest matters, because even the least presumptuousness is the greatest, is toward God. (CD-63)

55.   Presumptuousness therefore is *either* in a forbidden, a rebellious, an ungodly way *to want to have God's help*, or, in a forbidden, a rebellious, an ungodly way *to want to do without God's help*. (CD-63)

56.   If one were to charge them with being presumptuous toward God, they would no doubt answer, "That really never occurred to us." But precisely this is the presumptuousness, that it never occurred to them—to think about God. (CD-64)

57.   But the Christian knows that to need God is a human being's perfection. (CD-64)

58.   . . . One cannot kill God; on the other hand, as is said, one certainly can kill the thought of him. (CD-66)

59.   To slay God is the most dreadful suicide; utterly to forget God is a human being's deepest fall—a beast cannot fall that deep. (CD-67)

60. To grant God the victory, to comfort oneself because it is he who has been victorious—oh, that is basically to grant oneself the victory! In relation to God a person can truly be victorious only in this way, that God is victorious. (CD-126)

61. Thus love, which made the human being into something (omnipotence made him come into existence, but love made him come into existence *for* God), lovingly requires something of him. (CD-128)

62. God's greatness in nature is *manifest*, but God's greatness in showing mercy is a *mystery*, which must be believed. (CD-291)

63. . . . When I speak, there is a very exalted person listening—moreover, this is the case with every human being, but the majority do not bear it in mind—there is a very exalted person listening: God in heaven; he is in heaven and hears what every person says. (POV-190)

64. . . . Seventy years is not eternity. But the eternally Changeless One—suppose you are in disagreement with him—it is indeed an eternity: terrible! (M-273)

65. Ah, this human heart, what do you not hide in your secret inclosures, unknown to others—that would not be the worst—but at times almost unknown to the person himself! (M-277)

66. God's changelessness is blessed, indeed, who doubts that; just see to it that you become like that so that you can blessedly rest in this changelessness! . . . No one but you yourself can disturb this rest. (M-279)

Christ

67. God became flesh only once, and it is futile to expect that it could happen more than once. In paganism, it could happen frequently, but that was simply because it was not a true incarnation. Thus, a person is born only once, and there is no probability of a repetition. Transmigration of souls fails to appreciate the meaning of birth. (E/O II-40)

68. In Christ everything is revealed—and everything is hidden. (EUD-433)

69. Presumably it could occur to a human being to poetize himself in the likeness of the god or the god in the likeness of himself, but not to poetize that the god poetized himself in the likeness of a human being. (PF-36)

70. Christianity nevertheless always requires the confession of Christ . . . (CA-263)

71. To place a crown of thorns on his head and spit on him is blasphemy, but to make God so lofty that his existence becomes a delusion, becomes meaningless—that, too, is blasphemy. (UDVS-208)

72. . . . It was very dangerous . . . to ask Christ questions. The questioner did indeed always receive an answer, but in addition to the answer he in one sense learned too much. He received an imprisoning answer . . . (WOL-96)

73.   We do not believe that he [Christ, the prototype] came to the world in order to give us subjects for erudite research. He came to the world to set the task. (CD-76)

74.   When at one time they wanted to proclaim him king, he *fled*, and when they come armed to arrest him he *goes to meet* the sentry and says, "Whom do you seek?" (CD-277)

75.   . . . Never has the need for a redeemer been clearer than when the human race crucified the Redeemer. (CD-280)

76.   No, heaven will become weary of carrying the stars and will cast them away before he becomes weary of forgiving and thrusts the penitent away from himself. (CD-285)

77.   . . . "A cloud took him out of their sight," but the blessing remained behind. . . . But this, of course, is always how he is parted from his own—blessing them. . . . Just as that progenitor of the Hebrew people who wrestled with God said, "I will not let you go unless you bless me," so it is as though he says, "I will not leave you without blessing you." . . . (CD-296)

78.   There is something very upbuilding in the thought that what is said of Christ also holds true of all suffering: what he suffered he suffered once. One suffers only once: the victory is eternal. (CD-370)

79.   Oh, do not forget that there where he [Christ] is, there—in the spiritual sense—is the altar. (CD-392)

80. Lord Jesus Christ, you who certainly did not come to the world in order to judge, yet by being love that was not loved you were a judgment upon the world. (WA-169)

81. You were homeless in the world—yet you yourself were a hiding place, the only place where the sinner could flee. (WA-181)

82. The greatest possible human misery, greater even than sin, is to be offended at Christ and to continue in the offense; and Christ cannot, "love" cannot, make this impossible. (SUD-126)

83. Of course, in this denial of Christ as the paradox lies, in turn, the denial of all that is essentially Christian: sin, the forgiveness of sins, etc. . . . This offense is the highest intensification of sin, something that is usually overlooked because the opposites are not construed Christianly as being sin/faith. (SUD-131)

84. But that God has lived here on earth as an individual human being is infinitely extraordinary [noteworthy]. (PIC-31)

85. It is he who is the examiner; his life is the examination, and not for his generation alone, but for the human race. (PIC-34)

86. . . . If only one could trick his wisdom out of him— without becoming his follower! (PIC-44)

87. . . . The teacher is more important than the teaching. (PIC-123)

88. And if the God-man is abolished, Christianity is abolished. (PIC-144)

89. He came into the world in order to suffer; that he called being victorious. (PIC-224)

90. Neither by birth nor by external circumstances does he [Christ] belong to the mighty, but they see well enough that he *is* a power. (JFY-171)

91. In connection with all communication of truth, if it is supposed to be true, it must first be asked whether what is said is true, and next it must be asked who the speaker is, what does his life express. (JFY-178)

92. Christ's whole life here on earth would indeed have become a game if he had been so incognito that he had gone through life totally unnoticed—yet he truly was incognito. (POV-34)

93. But Christ is also much more than the prototype; he is the object of faith. (POV-131)

94. . . . Certainly about the most ludicrous [thing] it is possible to imagine: that God should let himself be *born*, that *the truth* should have entered into the world—in order to make banal remarks; and likewise a new difficulty, the difficulty of explaining that Christ then could be crucified, inasmuch as in this world of banality the death sentence is ordinarily not passed on the making of banal remarks. (M-221)

95. The God-man is betrayed, mocked, abandoned by all, all, all; not a single person, literally not one single one,

remains faithful to him—and then afterward, afterward, afterward there are millions who on their knees have made pilgrimages to the places where many hundreds of years ago his foot may have left a trace; afterward, afterward, afterward millions have worshiped a splinter of the cross on which he was crucified! . . . The only thing that Christ, the apostle, every truth-witness desire is: imitation—the only thing the human race has no pleasure in or taste for. (M-317)

96.   Only one thing did the Savior require; the same thing the apostle in turn after him and the truth-witness required as the one and only thing: imitation. (M-321)

97.   Christ is the prototype. This is true, and surely this is what must be particularly stressed in our time. But he still is not altogether literally the prototype, because he is, of course, heterogeneous to an ordinary human being by a full quality—and still he is the prototype. What does this mean? It means that in being the prototype he is also intended to teach us how greatly we need *grace*. (M-422)

II. MAN

Human Nature—Good

98.   Only responsibility gives a blessing and true joy. (E/O II-86)

99.   . . . It is greater to possess than to conquer. (E/O II-132)

100.   The healthy individual lives simultaneously in hope and in recollection . . . (E/O II-142)

101.   Philosophy has nothing at all to do with what could be called the inner deed, but the inner deed is the true life of freedom. Philosophy considers the external deed. (E/O II-174)

102.   . . . It takes great courage to do the ordinary . . . (E/O II-298)

103.   The genuinely extraordinary person is the genuinely ordinary person. The more of the universally human an individual can actualize in his life, the more extraordinary a human being he is. (E/O II-328)

104.   . . . To find the *idea* for which I am willing to live and die. (E/O II-361)

105.   If the human being is to rule, then there must be an order in the world; otherwise it would be mockery of him to assign him to control brute forces that obey no law. And if he is to rule, then there must be a law within him also; otherwise he would be incapable of ruling; either he would disturbingly interfere, or it would be left to chance whether he ruled wisely or not. (EUD-84)

106.   Or is it not something to make one shudder in a period of quiet, to make one feel faint in an odd moment—to have power and not know *for what purpose* one has it! (EUD-91)

107.   Among the many goods there is one that is the highest, that is not defined by its relation to the other goods, because it is the highest, and yet the person wishing does not have a definite idea of it, because it is the highest as the unknown . . . (TDIO-18)

108.   I would, however, rather be a concretion that means something than an abstraction that means everything. (SOLW-59)

109.   . . . Discourse about the natural changes of human life over the years as well as about what happens externally is not essentially different from discourse about plant or animal life. (UDVS-9)

110.   Therefore greatness of heart is the true human greatness, but greatness of heart is to master oneself in love. (CD-291)

111.   . . . Nature is pure symbol and pure instruction for man; it, too, is inspired by God and is "profitable for instruction, for reproof, for correction." (JFY-182)

112.   For goodness is to give oneself away completely, but in such a way that by omnipotently taking oneself back one makes the recipient independent. (M-391)

113.   It is incomprehensible that omnipotence is able not only to create the most impressive of all things—the whole visible world—but is able to create the most fragile of all things—a being independent of that very omnipotence. (M-391)

114. Only a wretched and worldly conception of the dialectic of power holds that it is greater and greater in proportion to its ability to compel and to make dependent. . . . The art of power lies precisely in making another free. (M-391)

Human Nature—Bad

115. . . . But the flesh is not the sensuous—it is the selfish. (E/O II-49)

116. It teaches "Enjoy life" and interprets it as "Live for your desire." But desire per se is a multiplicity . . . (E/O II-183)

117. To live in order to satisfy one's desire is a very distinguished appointment in life, and thank God one rarely sees it put into practice completely because of the trials and tribulations in life that give a person something else to think about. If this were not the case, we no doubt would often enough be witnesses to this terrible spectacle, for we certainly too frequently hear people complain that they feel cramped by their prosaic life, which unfortunately all too often means nothing else than that they would like to fling themselves into all the wildness into which desire can spin a person. (E/O-184)

118. Or what happens to a person who, in conflict with himself, does not confess that even if he were able to overcome everything he still would not have the power to overcome himself by himself! (EUD-128)

119.   You, who are evil . . . a truth decided once and for all and merely mentioned. (EUD-130)

120.   It could not occur to anyone to say about any subsequent man that by his first sin sinfulness came into the world; and yet it comes into the world by him in a similar way. (COA-33)

121.   Just as Adam lost innocence by guilt, so every man loses it in the same way. (COA-35)

122.   . . . It is certain from pagan as well as from Christian experience that man's desire is for the forbidden. (COA-40)

123.   . . . The fall. This is something that psychology is unable to explain, because the fall is the qualitative leap. (COA-48)

124.   . . . Sin has so often been explained a selfishness, precisely here lies the difficulty of finding a place for its explanation in any science. For selfishness is precisely the particular. (COA-77)

125.   Here sin, of course, signifies the concrete, for one never sins on the average or in general. (COA-114)

126.   The most terrible punishment for sin is the new sin. (COA-173)

127.   . . . All desire is selfish. (SOLW-42)

128.   The sins of the flesh are the self-willfulness of the lower self, but how often is not one devil driven out with the

devil's help and the last condition becomes worse than the first. . . . The opposite of sin is not virtue but faith. (SUD-82)

129.   Christianity has as its presupposition that the human race is a lost race, that everyone who is born, by being born, by thus belonging to the race, is a lost soul. (M-253)

Good and Evil

130.   The majority of people are willing to be grateful when they receive a good gift, but then they demand that it be left to them to decide which gift is good. (E/O II-98)

131.   Human thought knows the way to much in the world, . . . but the way to the good, to the secret hiding place of the good, this it does not know, since there is no way to it, but every good and every perfect gift comes *down* from above. (EUD-134)

132.   A person can be both good and evil, . . . but one cannot *simultaneously become* good and evil. (CUP-420)

133.   . . . The agonizing self-contradiction of worldly passion results from the individual's relating himself *absolutely* to a relative *telos*. (CUP-422)

134.   The distinction between good and evil is enervated by a loose, supercilious, theoretical acquaintance with evil, by an overbearing shrewdness which knows that the good is not appreciated or rewarded in the world—and thus it practically becomes stupidity. (TA-78)

135.   Force can be used against rebellion, punishment awaits demonstrable counterfeiting, but dialectical secretiveness is difficult to root out; it takes relatively more acute ears to track down the muffled steps of reflection stealing down the furtive corridors of ambiguity and equivocation. (TA-80)

136.   If a person is to will the good in truth, he must make up his mind to will to renounce all double-mindedness. (UDVS-35)

137.   . . . The person who wills the good for the sake of reward does not will one thing but is double-minded. . . . It is really the same as if a person, instead of doing what is natural, using both eyes to look at one thing, were to use one eye to look to the one side and the other to look to the other side—it will not work, it only confuses the vision. (UDVS-37)

138.   . . . The person who wills the good only out of fear of punishment does not will one thing but is double-minded. (UDVS-44)

139.   He should fear doing wrong; but if he has done wrong, then, if he actually wills one thing and wills the good in truth, he must even desire to be punished so that the punishment can heal him just as the medicine heals the sick . . . (UDVS-45)

140.   . . . When someone wills to do the good out of fear of punishment . . . it can be like . . . the fearful person's reducing his life to sheer sickliness out of fear of becoming sick . . . (UDVS-45)

141.   Fear of physical debility has certainly taught the profligate to observe moderation in his debauchery . . . but it has never made him chaste. . . . It taught him to mock God daily by moderation—in debauchery (abominable composure!). (UDVS-46)

142.   But someone who wills the good in truth understands that the punishment exists only on account of the transgressions; he devoutly understands that the punishment is like everything else that befalls one who loves God— a helping hand. (UDVS-51)

143.   . . . The punishment God in his wisdom has attached to every transgression is a good, but it is that only when it is received with gratitude, not when it is only feared as an evil . . . (UDVS-56)

144.   . . . The good and the world's punishment are not homogeneous. (UDVS-56)

145.   In the motley, teeming crowd, in the noise of the world, little attention is paid from day to day and year to year to whether a person completely wills the good if only he has influence and power, is in a big enterprise, is somebody to himself and to others. . . . It is not such a scrupulous matter whether a person completely wills the good—as long as he is enterprising, not to mention a thief, in his job, as long as he saves and accumulates, as long as he has a good reputation and, incidentally, avoids scandal . . . (UDVS-66)

146.   If a person is to will the good in truth, he must will to do everything for the good or will to suffer everything for the good. (UDVS-78)

147. The good is not aristocratic; it asks for neither more nor less than everything, whether this is a little bit or not makes no difference. (UDVS-84)

148. If a person is to will the good in truth, he must will to suffer everything for the good. . . . In the decision he must will to be and to remain with the good. (UDVS-99)

149. [One] is not eternally responsible for achieving his end in temporality, but [one] is unconditionally eternally responsible for which means he uses. (UDVS-141)

150. But if you have asked God for help, then you are bound, bound to accept the help as he sees fit. How often we hear this cry for help and this cry that there is no help—truly, there is always sufficient help. But the human heart is so cunning and has so little fidelity to its word that, when the help proves to be what one most feared, one says, "But that certainly is not help!" But if this help is from God and if you have asked him for help, then you are committed to accepting the help and in faith and gratitude to call it help. (CD-168)

151. "Blessedness" is certainly the highest good . . . (CD-222)

152. What is the only distinction God makes? The one between right and wrong. (CD-224)

153. What then is the blessing? The blessing is God's consent to the undertaking that a person prays God to bless. And what does it mean that he prays for the blessing? It means that he dedicates himself and his undertaking to

serving God—regardless of whether or not it, humanly speaking, succeeds or progresses. (CD-297)

154.   . . . If divine justice, punishing, quickly intervened, the really capital crimes could not completely come into existence. (M-304)

155.   Therefore never complain when you see the success of something terrible that will rouse your indignation against God; do not complain—no, tremble and say: God in heaven, so he is one of the capital criminals whose crime needs all of temporal life to come into existence and is not punished until eternity. Therefore it is precisely severity that brings it about that the capital crime is not punished in this world. (M-305)

156.   Men are not so corrupt that they actually wish to do evil, but they are blinded, and don't really know what they are doing. (D-105)

Kierkegaard the Author

157.   To be an author in Denmark is almost as troublesome as having to live in public view . . . (P-15)

158.   The forces of the reading public are concentrated in Copenhagen, and yet this concentration has nothing to do with strength but only with uproar and noise and racket and officious busyness in all external endeavors. (P-15)

159.   . . . Empty barrels make the greatest sound and the synagogue [a popular restaurant favored by the intelligentsia],

like the church bell, has—a tongue and an empty head. If one wants to make visible to the eye what here is presented mostly to the ear, then one sees the multitude of the reading public crowded together at the alarm center. All are milling around in total confusion. If one looks more closely, one notices a few characters who are differentiated from the crowd. By their watchful gaze, their restless glances, their outstretched necks, their perked up ears, one easily identifies them—they are the reviewers. Perhaps you think that a reviewer is to be looked upon as a police inspector in the service of good taste. You are mistaken. A reviewer is a conspirator, a worthy member of the Intemperance Association. When he has heard what he wants, he then rushes home, and while the empty chatter is still rattling in his head, he writes a review. A fortnight later, the visible reading public (there is a distinction, like that between the visible and invisible Church) is gathered again in the synagogue. People begin where they left off. "Have you read the superb review?" No. "Then you must read it. You must be sure to read it; it is exactly as I myself could have written it."—"Strangely enough, what the interesting reviewer says is the same as what I said when I had just paged through the book at Reitzel's." [bookstore named after the owner who also published many of Kierkegaard's books]—And I have not read it yet, but I heard from a friend out in the country, who has a damned good head and is a connoisseur, that the book falls short, even though there are some beautiful passages in it."—It is linked together in the following way. That friend out in the country has not read the book but received a letter from a man in the capital who has not read the book either but read the review that in turn was written by a man who had not read the book but heard what that trustworthy man said who had paged through it a little at Reitzel's. (P-16)

160.	To write a book is the easiest of all things in our time, if, as is customary, one takes ten older works on the same subject and out of them puts together an eleventh on the same subject. (P-35)

161.	. . . Awareness of one's own unworthiness does not promptly give a person the courage to admit to himself and others the truth of the matter. (CA-3)

162.	To be called before the front line of the reading public to be commended—ah, yes! But then it must be the general who does it. If the summoner, for example, is the driver of an ammunition wagon, then both become ridiculous. (CA-25)

163.	Unwarranted recognition is just as objectionable as an unwarranted attack. (CA-26)

164.	. . . A woman told me that I look splendid from a distance. (CA-85)

165.	I have always regarded pseudonymity as a bill of divorcement between an author and his work . . . (CA-156)

166.	[In addressing the Corsair] Slay me so I may live with all the others you have slain, but do not slay me by making me immortal. (CA-158)

167.	The public mind is prodigiously developed in Denmark. Murder, prostitution, violence, in short, every crime is forgiven except the crime of having different buttons on one's coat than other men have. (CA-224)

168.   A martyrdom of laughter is what I really have suffered. (CA-236)

169.   I have a university degree—it is not much, it is not for that reason that I speak of it—but I merely state that it is not by first seeking the kingdom of God that I became an M.A. [Magister, Master's degree] (JFY-250)

170.   "Without authority" to make aware of the religious, the essentially Christian, is the category for my whole work as an author regarded as a totality. (POV-12)

171.   . . . I am and was a religious author, that my whole authorship pertains to Christianity, to the issue: becoming a Christian, with direct [author's name attached] and indirect [pseudonymous] polemical aim at the enormous illusion, Christendom, or the illusion that in such a country all are Christians of sorts. (POV-23)

172.   The religious is present from the very beginning. Conversely, the esthetic is still present even in the last moment. . . . The first division of books is esthetic writing; the last division of books is exclusively religious writing—between these lies *Concluding Unscientific Postscript* as the *turning point*. This work deals with and poses *the issue*, the issue of the entire work as an author: becoming a Christian (POV-31)

173.   . . . An illusion can never be removed directly, and basically only indirectly. If it is an illusion that all are Christians, and if something is to be done, it must be done

indirectly, not by someone who loudly declares himself to be an extraordinary Christian, but by someone who better informed, even declares himself not to be a Christian. That is, one who is under an illusion must be approached from behind. (POV-43)

174.   Generally speaking, there is nothing that requires as gentle a treatment as the removal of an illusion. If one in any way causes the one ensnared to be antagonized, then all is lost. And this one does by a direct attack. (POV-43)

175.   If one is truly to succeed in leading a person to a specific place, one must first and foremost take care to find him where *he* is and begin there. (POV-45)

176.   The helper must first humble himself under the person he wants to help and thereby understand that to help is not to dominate but to serve . . . (POV-45)

177.   If you can do it, if you can very accurately find the place where the other person is and begin there, then you can perhaps have the good fortune of leading him to the place where you are. (POV-46)

178.   A triumphant religious author who is *in vogue* is *eo ipso* not a *religious* author. The essentially religious author is always polemical and in addition suffers under the opposition or endures the opposition that corresponds to what in his time must be regarded as the specific evil. (POV-67)

179.   It holds for everyone that when he comes to death's door and it is opened for him he must discard all pomp and

glory and wealth and worldly esteem and starred medals and emblems of honor . . . —discard them as totally irrelevant and superfluous. An exception is made only for anyone who has been a religious author, teacher, speaker, etc. in his lifetime and has been that on his own responsibility and at his own risk. If he is found to be in possession of any such thing, he is not allowed to discard it—no, it is packed up in a bundle and handed to him; he is compelled to keep it or to carry the bundle in the same way as a thief is himself compelled to carry stolen goods. And with this bundle he must enter the place where he shall be judged. (POV-68)

180. The question of whether I am a Christian (and thus for every individual, whether he is a Christian) is entirely a God-relationship. (POV-135)

181. The more inwardness, the greater the fear and trembling before God. (POV-136)

182. . . . In Denmark one lives happily only when one is nobody. (POV-156)

183. God in heaven, who has reason to be disgusted with me because I am a sinner, has nevertheless not rejected what I, humanly speaking, honestly intended. Yet before God even my best deed is still miserable. (POV-161)

184. It has generally been thought that reflection is the natural enemy of Christianity and would destroy it. With God's help I hope to show that God-fearing reflection can retie knots that a shallow, superficial reflection has diddled with so long. (POV-167)

185.   Religiously the task was to move from the interesting and to arrive at the simple. (POV-262)

186.   What do I care about the world's honor and glory, and what do I care about its ridicule and scorn, indeed, what do I care about myself if only God may be honored. (POV-272)

The Individual

187.   . . . I myself am the absolute, because I myself can choose absolutely and this absolute choice of myself is my freedom. (E/O II-224)

188.   The phrase "know yourself" is a stock phrase, and in it has been perceived the goal of all a person's striving. . . . But . . . it cannot be the goal if it is not also the beginning. . . . And this is why I have with aforethought used the expression "to choose oneself" instead of "to know oneself." (E/O II-258)

189.   The single individual can mean the most unique of all and it can mean everyone. (EUD-475)

190.   The dialectic of antiquity was oriented to the eminent; . . . the dialectic of Christianity is oriented to representation. . . . The dialectic of the present age is oriented to equality, and its most logical implementation, albeit abortive, is leveling, the negative unity of the negative mutual reciprocity of individuals. (TA-84)

191.   The individual does not belong to God, to himself, to the beloved, to his art, to his scholarship; no, just as a

serf belongs to an estate, so the individual realizes that in every respect he belongs to an abstraction in which reflection subordinated him. (TA-85)

192. For it is extremely comic to see the particular individual classed under the infinite abstraction "pure humanity." . . . (TA-88)

193. That is the basest kind of leveling, because it always corresponds to the denominator in relation to which all are made equal. Thus eternal life is also a kind of leveling, and yet it is not so, for the denominator is this: to be an essentially human person in the religious sense. (TA-96)

194. . . . The person . . . exists only in an external sense as long as he lives a number in the crowd, [as] a fraction in a worldly complex . . . (UDVS-127)

195. But the Omniscient One, even though he surely can maintain an overview better than anyone else, does not want the crowd. He wants only the single individual . . . (UDVS-127)

196. Each human being, as a single individual, must account for himself to God . . . (UDVS-127)

197. . . . In eternity it will not be asked whether it was your wife who seduced you (eternity will discuss that with your wife), but you will only be asked as a single individual whether you allowed yourself to be seduced. (UDVS-130)

198.   . . . Untruth usually is numbers; truth is content with being a unity. (UDVS-132)

199.   Eternity, however, does not count; the single individual is continually only one, and the conscience keeps close watch on the single individual. In eternity you will look around in vain for the crowd . . . (UDVS-132)

200.   . . . Many fools do not make one wise man, and the crowd is a dubious recommendation for a cause. The bigger the crowd, the more likely that what it praises is foolishness, the less likely that it is truth, and the least likely that it is any eternal truth, because eternally, of course, there simply is no crowd at all. (UDVS-133)

201.   . . . In eternity you will be asked as a single individual only about your faith and about your faithfulness. There will be no question at all about whether you were in charge of much or little . . . (UDVS-147)

202.   Each one is alone as a single individual before God; husband and wife, even though they go together *to* confession, nevertheless do not confess together, because the person who is confessing is not in company; he is as a single individual alone before God. (UDVS-151)

203.   Only the single individual can will the good in truth . . . (UDVS-153)

204.   . . . When the Gospel speaks, it speaks to the single individual . . . (WOL-14)

205.   . . . To have a self, to be a self, is the greatest concession, an infinite concession, given to man, but it is also eternity's claim upon him. (SUD-21)

206.   . . . The self in despair wants to be master of itself or to create itself, to make his self into the self he wants to be, to determine what he will have or not have in his concrete self. . . . If a generic name for this despair is wanted, it could be called stoicism . . . (SUD-68)

207.   He will not first ask you, you suffering one—alas, as righteous people do even when they are willing to help: You are not yourself to blame for your trouble, are you? (PIC-19)

208.   Christianity did not enter into the world in order to reassure you in your natural condition, . . . but . . . it, renouncing all things, entered into the world in order, with the terrors of eternity, to wrest you out of the peace in which you naturally are. (M-312)

209.   Man almost never avails himself of his freedoms, freedom of thought, for instance; instead he demands freedom of speech. (D-17)

210.   But it is a paralogism that one thousand human beings are worth more than one. . . . The central point about being human is that the unit "1" is the highest; "1000" counts for less. (D-103)

211.   What I really lack is to be clear in my mind *what I am to do, not* what I am to know. Except in so far as a certain understanding must precede every action. The thing is to understand myself, to see what God really wishes me to do; the thing is to find a truth which is true *for me,* to find *the idea for which I can live and die.* . . . What good would it do me to be able to explain the meaning of Christianity if it had no deeper significance for me and for my life . . . *Journal,* Aug 1, 1835 (KA-4)

The Individual and the Crowd

212.   It is not enough that Cain was the first fratricide, no, he was also the first to build a city, and consequently from him came the desperate idea to pack people together in huge cities like herring in barrels. Cain, Cain, what have you done! (CA-80)

213.   . . . If individuals relate to an idea merely *en masse* (consequently without the individual separation of inwardness), we get violence, anarchy, riotousness; but if there is no idea for the individuals *en masse* and no individually separating essential inwardness, either, then we have crudeness. The harmony of the spheres is the unity of each planet relating to itself and to the whole. Take away the relations, and there will be chaos. (TA-63)

214.   Nowadays it is possible actually to speak with people, and what they say is admittedly very sensible, and yet the conversation leaves the impression that one has been speaking with an anonymity. (TA-103)

215.   Now everyone can have an opinion, but there must be a lumping together numerically in order to have it. (TA-106)

216.   . . . The generation has eliminated individualities and all the organic concretions and has substituted humanity and numerical equality among men . . . (TA-108)

217.   These servants of leveling are the servants of the power of evil, for leveling itself is not of God . . . (TA-109)

218.   . . . The most pernicious of all evasions—hidden in the crowd, to want as it were, to avoid God's inspection of oneself as a single individual, avoid hearing God's voice as a single individual . . . (UDVS-128)

219.   . . . The solitary voice is so easily outvoted—by the majority. But in eternity the conscience is the only voice heard. (UDVS-129)

220.   Or do you filter yourself into the crowd, where the one blames another, where at one moment there are, as they say, a *great many*, and where at the next moment, every time responsibility is mentioned, there is *no one*? (UDVS-131)

221.   . . . Individuals, when they forget the relation to God, become mutually afraid of one another; the single individual becomes afraid of the more or of the many, who in turn, each one out of fear of people and forgetting God, stick together and form the crowd, which renounces the nobility of eternity that is granted to each and every one—to be an individual. (UDVS-327)

222.   When the congregation gathers in great numbers on the festival days, he [God] knows them also, and those he does not know are not his own. . . . There is no crowd at the Communion table. (CD-272)

223.   One can point physically to the Communion table and say, "See, there it is," but in the spiritual sense the Communion table is *there* only if you are *known there* by him. (CD-273)

224.   The crowd, of course, cannot judge whether something
        is well worked out or not; it sticks to—the illusion.
        (CD-316)

225.   . . . Humankind resembles children in the marketplace,
        when they perceive that they have something and are
        permitted to keep it, they become ungrateful, and if not
        plainly ungrateful, then at least lazy in the habit of ad-
        miration. (CD-317)

226.   . . . There is in a *religious sense* no public but only indi-
        viduals. (POV-10)

227.   The crowd has no ideality and therefore no power to
        hold on to an idea despite appearances; the crowd al-
        ways falls into the trap of appearances. (POV-58)

228.   One must see how no attack is so feared as that of laugh-
        ter, how even the person who courageously risked his
        life for a stranger would not be far from betraying his
        father and mother if the danger was laughter, because
        more than any other this attack isolates the one attacked
        and at no point does it offer the support of pathos . . .
        (POV-65)

229.   . . . The political begins on earth in order to remain on
        earth, while the religious, taking its beginning from
        above, wants to transfigure and then to lift the earthly
        to heaven. (POV-103)

230.   But anyone who is to effect something must know his
        age—and then have the courage to risk the danger of
        using the surest means. (POV-115)

231. *The single individual* is the category of spirit, of spiritual awakening, as diametrically opposite to politics as possible. (POV-121)

232. There is a view of life that holds that truth is where the crowd is, that truth itself needs to have the crowd on its side. (POV-153)

233. To be sure, the crowd is formed by individuals, but each one must retain the power to remain what he is—an individual. (POV-153)

234. The single individual—with this category the cause of Christianity stands or falls. . . . Without this category, pantheism would be unconditionally victorious. (POV-155)

235. . . . To learn what it actually means to govern, that it is, in the fear of God, the responsibility to be strong and powerful enough not to fear people and "number," that it is in self-denial not to love governing but to love *the neighbor*, the true humanity and the true human equality. (POV-270)

236. . . . The first condition for entering into relation with people is that they be split apart. This again, is why great crimes make the relation more possible than mediocrity does, because great crimes isolate. (M-460)

237. . . . To form crowds is precisely the way to get rid of ideals. (M-460)

238. One must strengthen oneself religiously by the relation to God; from him strength will come, and not by forming parties, by becoming a lot of people etc. (M-540)

III. Man the Thinker

Truth

239. . . . There comes a midnight hour when every one must unmask . . . (E/O II-160)

240. What, then, should we call such a teacher who gives him the condition [the ability to understand truth] again and along with it the truth? Let us call him a *savior*. . . . Let us call him a *deliverer*, for he does indeed deliver the person who had imprisoned himself, and no one is so dreadfully imprisoned, and no captivity is so impossible to break out of as that in which the individual holds himself captive! (PF-17)

241. . . . That truth is for the particular individual only as he himself produces it in action. Truth has always had many loud proclaimers, but the question is whether a person will in the deepest sense acknowledge the truth, will allow it to permeate his whole being, will accept all its consequences, and not have an emergency hiding place for himself and a Judas kiss for the consequence. (COA-138)

242. Alas, yet it is so easy, so very easy, to acquire a true opinion, and yet it is so difficult, so very difficult, to have an opinion and to have it in truth. (TDIO-100)

243. Honor be to learning and knowledge; praised be the one who masters the material with the certainty of knowledge, with the reliability of autopsy. (CUP-11)

244. In relation to an eternal truth that is supposed to be decisive for an eternal happiness, eighteen centuries have no greater demonstrative weight than a single day. (CUP-47)

245. . . . It surely is an even more dreadful untruth to leave God, if I dare to put it this way, continually out of the picture and thus to take comfort because one has not been sentenced for anything . . . (CUP-542)

246. They are busy obtaining a truer and truer conception of God but seem to forget the first basic principle: that one ought to fear God. (CUP-544)

247. We can be deceived by believing what is untrue, but we certainly are also deceived by not believing what is true. (WOL-5)

248. How many an individual has not asked, "What is truth?" and at bottom hoped that it would be a long time before the truth would come so close to him that in the same instant it would determine what it was his duty to do at that moment. (WOL-96)

249. He walks on and on like the person who walks along a road that the passersby tell him definitely leads to the city but forget to tell him that if we wants to go to the city he must turn around; he is walking along the road that leads to the city, is walking along the road—away from the city. (CD-39)

250. The youth *says what is true*, but the old man has verified it, *has made true* that which is indeed eternally true. (CD-98)

251. . . . One has in one's innermost being a secret anxiety about and wariness of the truth, a fear of getting to know too much. Or do you actually believe that it is everyone's honest desire to get to know very effectually what self-denial is, to get it made so clear that every excuse, every evasion, every extenuation, every refuge in the false but favorable opinion of others is cut off for him! Do you believe this? Well, I need not wait for your answer . . . (CD-170)

252. Take care, therefore, when you go up to the house of the Lord, because there you will get to hear the truth—for upbuilding. (CD-171)

253. And in the house of the Lord you get to know the truth that you must die to the world, and if God has found that you have learned this, then in all eternity no escape will help you. (CD-172)

254. If a liar were to say, "Get involved with me, fight me with my own weapons," could truth be served with this proposal or with winning such a victory! (CD-190)

255. Alas, we human beings, even if we are of *the truth*, are still alongside the truth; when we walk side by side with the man who is *the Truth*, when *the Truth* is the criterion, we are still like children alongside a giant . . . (CD-278)

256. Thus Christ is the truth in the sense that to be the truth is the only true explanation of what truth is. (PIC-205)

257. Christianly understood, truth is obviously not to know the truth but to be the truth. (PIC-205)

258. But when the truth itself is the way, then the way cannot be shortened or drop out unless the truth is distorted or it drops out. (PIC-207)

259. . . . Spiritually understood, the human being in his natural state is sick, he is in error, in a self-deception. Therefore he craves most of all to be deceived; then he is allowed not only to remain in error but to feel really at home in the self-deception. (M-224)

260. If you want to take care for your eternal future, see to it that you come to suffer for the truth. . . . Perhaps you are contemporary with a *righteous person* who suffers for the truth—here, then, is the opportunity: acknowledge him for what he is and you will come to suffer like him! (M-298)

261. . . . "The truth" has, if I may say it this way, a pen in its hand; it writes on a little slip of paper "for eternity." . . . (M-299)

262. There is a view of life that holds that truth is where the crowd is, that truth itself needs to have the crowd on its side. There is another view of life that holds that wherever the crowd is, untruth is, so that even if—to carry the matter to its ultimate for a moment—all individuals who, separately, secretly possessed the truth were to come together in a crowd (in such a way, however, that

"the crowd" acquired any *deciding*, voting, noisy, loud significance), untruth would promptly be present there. (POV-106)

263. The crowd is untruth. (POV-108)

264. The truth can neither be communicated nor be received without being, as it were, under the eyes of God, without the help of God, without God's being a participant, the middle term, since God is the truth. Therefore it can be communicated by and received only by *the single individual*, who as a matter of fact could be every person who is living. (POV-111)

265. If everyone in truth loved the neighbor as himself, then perfect human equality would be achieved unconditionally. (POV-111)

266. But I have never read in Holy Scripture this commandment: You shall love the crowd, to say nothing of: ethically-religiously you are to recognize the crowd as the authority with regard to *the truth*. But to love the neighbor is, of course, self-denial; to love the crowd or pretend to love it, to make it the authority for *the truth*, is the way to acquire tangible power, the way to all kinds of temporal and worldly advantage—it is also untruth, since the crowd is untruth. (POV-111)

267. *At the base* of all *actual disagreement*, there is an understanding; the *baselessness* of *misunderstanding* is that the preliminary understanding is lacking, without which both agreement and disagreement are a misunderstanding. A misunderstanding, therefore, can be removed and become agreement and understanding, but is can also

be removed and become actual disagreement. That two people are actually in disagreement is no misunderstanding—they are actually in disagreement simply because they do understand each other. (POV-113)

268.   . . . An eternal truth that from first to last is equally true, no more true in its latest moment than in its first . . . (BOA-36)

269.   Truth indirectly makes untruth manifest. (BOA-220)

270.   There is only one relation to revealed truth: to have faith [believe it]. That one has faith can be demonstrated in only one way: by being willing to suffer for one's faith; and the degree of one's faith is demonstrated only by the degree of one's willingness to suffer for one's faith. (M-324)

Reason

271.   . . . Every speculative thinker confuses himself with humankind, whereby he becomes something infinitely great and nothing at all. (CUP-124)

272.   The existential expression of nullifying the principle of contradiction is to be in contradiction to oneself. (TA-97)

273.   But it must always be kept in mind that reflection itself is not something pernicious . . . (TA-110)

274.   . . . Christianity is indeed something essentially and completely different from a science like mathematics etc.,

which is indifferent to the personal, and that Christianity is least of all brought to its highest when, homogeneous with the world, it is lectured upon by secularly successful assistant professors as an objective science or when . . . the decision to become a Christian . . . is put off, because one is continually expecting—a conclusion from scientific scholarship. (JFY-195)

275.   . . . They tried to demonstrate the truth of Christianity with reasons or by advancing reasons in relation to Christianity. And these reasons fostered doubt and doubt became the stronger. The demonstration of Christianity really lies in *imitation*. (FSE-68)

Life's Goal

276.   Andersen totally lacks a life view. . . . For a life-view is more than a quintessence or a sum of propositions maintained in its abstract neutrality; it is more than experience, which as such is always fragmentary. It is, namely, the transubstantiation of experience; it is an unshakable certainty in oneself won from all experience, whether this has oriented itself only in all worldly relationships (a purely human standpoint, Stoicism, for example), by which means it keeps itself from contact with a deeper experience—or whether in its heavenward direction (the religious) it has found therein the center as much for its heavenly as its earthly existence, has won the true Christian conviction "that neither death, nor life, nor angels, nor principalities, nor powers, nor the present, nor the future, nor height, nor depth, nor any other creation will be able to separate us from the love of God in Christ Jesus our Lord." . . . On

the other hand single propositions stick out like hieroglyphs that at times are the object of a pious veneration. (EPW-76)

277. On the one hand it is taught that on every person there is written a *mene mene* etc. In analogy to this, individuals appear whose actual task lies behind them, but this does not help them to come into the right "backward" position for viewing life, since this task is placed rather like a hump on their own backs, and therefore they never actually come to see it or could never possibly become conscious of it in a spiritual sense . . . (EPW-77)

278. A life-view is really providence in the novel; it is its deeper unity, which makes the novel have the center of gravity in itself. A life-view frees it from being arbitrary or purposeless, since the purpose is immanently present everywhere in the work of art. (EPW-81)

279. Prosperity is what is helpful to me in reaching my goal, what leads me to my goal; and adversity is what will prevent me from reaching my goal. (CD-151)

280. Only the one who has the true conception of what the goal is that is set before human beings, only he knows also what adversity is and what prosperity is. (CD-152)

281. . . . There are only two goals: one goal that a person desires, craves to reach, and the other that he should reach. (CD-152)

282. . . . When by means of prosperity he reaches temporality's goal, he is furthest away from reaching *the goal*. (CD-154)

283.   . . . You [with no possessions] have only the task *of renouncing what has been denied you*, whereas he [with possessions] has the task *of renouncing what has been given to him*. . . . You are denied what will prevent you from reaching *the goal* . . . (CD-157)

284.   One certainly does not have religion for the sake of this life, in order to get through this life happy and well, but for the sake of the other life; in this other world lies the earnestness of religion. (M-312)

IV. THE CHRISTIAN LIFE

Faith / Faithfulness

285.   . . . It is easy enough to say that God is greatest in the least, but to be able to see him there takes the strongest faith. (E/O II-285)

286.   Faith . . . is not only the highest good, but it is a good in which all are able to share . . . (EUD-10)

287.   . . . And every human being has it if he wants to have it—it is precisely the gloriousness of faith that it can be had only on this condition. (EUD-14)

288.   He [Abraham] had faith by virtue of the absurd, for all human calculation ceased long ago. (FAT-35)

289.   . . . He who loves God without faith reflects upon himself; he who loves God in faith reflects upon God. (FAT-37)

290. Faith is namely this paradox that the single individual is higher than the universal . . . (FAT-55)

291. The paradox of faith, then, is this: that the single individual is higher than the universal, that the single individual . . . determines his relation to the universal by his relation to the absolute, not his relation to the absolute by his relation to the universal. (FAT-70)

292. The tragic hero relinquishes himself in order to express the universal; the knight of faith relinquishes the universal in order to become the single individual. (FAT-75)

293. Faith loses by being regarded as the immediate, since it has been deprived of what lawfully belongs to it, namely, its historical presupposition. (COA-10)

294. Without risk, no faith. . . . If I am able to apprehend God objectively, I do not have faith; but because I cannot do this, I must have faith. (CUP-204)

295. Faith says: Everything is forgotten, but remember that it is forgiven. . . . Eternal justice can and will forget in only one way, through forgiveness . . . (UDVS-247)

296. What is easier to understand than: when I gain everything, I lose nothing at all? Only when it must be believed does the difficulty actually arise. (CD-146)

297. To understand it is easy enough—but to believe it is difficult. . . . As long as you do not believe it, it is not true for you. (CD-157)

298.   But if you selected one single person whom you made the object of all your attention—you cannot know whether he is a believer; you can know only that he affirms it. (CD-237)

299.   Faith's question . . . is to *you*: Have *you* believed? (CD-238)

300.   The one clause is rigorous [If we deny, he also will deny us], the other lenient [he remains faithful; he cannot deny himself]—in fact, here there is Law and Gospel, but both clauses are the truth. . . . So that we [may] at no time separate what God has joined together in Christ, neither add anything nor subtract anything, do not subtract the rigorousness from the leniency that is in them, do not subtract from the Gospel the Law that is in it, do not subtract from the salvation the perdition that is in it . . . (CD-283)

301.   Humanly speaking, in the relation between two people, each of them always has a dual concern; he has the one for himself, that he will remain faithful, but in addition has the one about whether the other will also remain faithful. But he, Jesus Christ, he remains faithful. In this relationship, therefore, the peace and blessedness of eternity is complete; you have only one concern, the self-concern that you remain faithful to Christ—for he remains eternally faithful. (CD-284)

302.   If in the relationship between two people one became unfaithful but repented of his unfaithfulness and returned—alas, perhaps his unfaithfulness would have had the power to change the other person so that he could not bring himself to forgive him. But he, our Lord Jesus Christ, remains faithful to himself. (CD-285)

303. Alas, complete faithfulness was never found in the world—if anyone was at all justified in seeking it in others. But complete faithfulness in return for faithlessness, that is found only with our heavenly teacher and friend—and surely we all need to seek that. (CD-286)

304. . . . We know very well that *fundamentally* we are faithless and that at every moment and *fundamentally* it is you who are holding on to us. (CD-286)

305. The confession does not want to burden you with the guilt of faithlessness; on the contrary, it wants to help you, through confession, to lay aside the burden. (CD-287)

306. To what end has faith, which you say you have, made you restless, where have you witnessed for the truth, where against untruth, what sacrifices have you made, what persecution have you suffered for your Christianity, and at home in your domestic life where have your self-denial and renunciation been noticeable? (FSE-18)

Work(s)

307. . . . The weed of corruption has the characteristic that all weeds have; it sows itself. The good seed requires care and work, and if that is lacking the good seed perishes—and then the weeds come by themselves. (TDIO-55)

308. So where does a person find guidance if he himself does not work out his own soul's salvation in fear and trembling . . .? (TDIO-61)

309. . . . The lazy person always has an inordinate imagination; he promptly thinks of how he is going to arrange things for himself and how comfortable he will be as soon as this and that are done; he thinks less about the fact that it is this and that which he is to do. (UDVS-73)

310. To work is a human being's perfection. By working, human beings resemble God, who indeed also works. (UDVS-198)

311. Oh, in the customary pursuits of daily life, how easy it is, in the spiritual sense, to doze off . . . (CD-254)

312. . . . The more you become involved with God, the clearer it will be how much less you yourself are capable of doing . . . . At the Communion table you are capable of doing nothing at all. (CD-298)

313. At the Communion table you are capable of less than nothing. . . . You cannot meet him before the Communion table as a co-worker as you indeed can meet God in your work as a co-worker. (CD-299)

314. Christianity's requirement is this: your life should express works as strenuously as possible; then one thing more is required—that you humble yourself and confess: But my being saved is nevertheless grace. (FSE-17)

315. Good works are something like a dish which is that particular dish because of the way in which it is served—likewise good works should be served in humility, in faith. Or it is like a child's giving his parents a present,

purchased, however, with what the child has received from his parents . . . (M-392)

Christendom

316. How can you not be a Christian? You are Danish, aren't you? Doesn't the geography book say that the predominant religion in Denmark is Lutheran-Christian? (CUP-50)

317. Once Christianity was an offense to the Jews and foolishness to the Greeks, and now it is—culture. For Bishop Mynster the mark of true Christianity is culture. (CA-257)

318. Christianity teaches that a danger is involved, persecution goes along with confessing that one is a true Christian . . . (CA-262)

319. The word "Christendom" as a general designation for a whole nation is a caption that easily says too much and thus in turn prompts the single individual to believe too much about himself. (WOL-48)

320. . . . The pagans who are found in Christendom have sunk the lowest. Those in the pagan countries have not as yet been lifted up to Christianity; the pagans in Christendom have sunk below paganism. (CD-12)

321. But I certainly do feel alienated in Christendom insofar as all Christendom is supposed to be only Christians, more alienated than if I lived among pagans. A person cannot be as alienated by the indifference to his faith

on the part of those who have another faith, another God, as he must feel alienated by the indifference of those who say they have the same faith—to the same faith. (CD-243)

322. For a person to be a Christian, it certainly is required that what he believes is a *definite* something, but then with equal certainty it is also required that it be *entirely definite* that *he* believes. (CD-244)

323. . . . We do indeed live in Christian countries, but just as one often enough sees examples of esthetic bestiality, so, too, the cannibalistic taste for human sacrifices has far from become obsolete in Christendom. (CD-304)

324. What communism makes such a big fuss about, Christianity accepts as something that is self-evident, that all people are equal before God, therefore essentially equal. (CD-383)

325. In Christendom he is a Christian (in the very same sense as in paganism he would be a pagan and in Holland a Hollander), one of the cultured Christians. (SUD-56)

326. For people are willing enough to practice compassion and self-denial, willing enough to seek after wisdom, etc., but they want to determine the criterion themselves, that it shall be to a certain degree. (PIC-60)

327. But woe, woe to the Christian Church when it will have been victorious in this world, for then it is not the Church that has been victorious but the world. Then the heterogeneity between Christianity and the world

has vanished, the world has won, and Christianity has lost. Then Christ is no longer the God-man but a distinguished human being whose life is related homogeneously to the development of the human race. (PIC-223)

328.   And the day when Christianity and the world become friends—yes, then Christianity is abolished. (PIC-224)

329.   . . . But Christianity is abolished as soon as it is thrust from the throne. Christianity is the unconditioned, has only one being, unconditioned being . . . either/or applies unconditionally. (PIC-227)

330.   . . . Established Christendom became a collection of what could be called honorary Christians in the same sense as we speak of honorary doctors, who receive their degrees without having written and defended a doctoral dissertation . . . . There arose in Christendom a class of Christians that is so odd that it could be exhibited for money. In the course of time, namely, there appeared in Christendom atheists and people of that mentality who attacked, ridiculed, and mocked Christianity worse than the worst pagan mockers had done. But since these people were born in Christendom, lived in Christendom where all, of course, are Christians, and since they presumably did not find it worth their trouble. Or perhaps found it too great a sacrifice to make, to relinquish the name "Christian", and since CHRISTENDOM, no doubt because of its extraordinary expansion, had lost the resiliency to shake from itself Christians of that sort, these people went on calling themselves Christians and people went on calling them Christians. (PIC-253)

331. Indeed, the Church did not decline, decrease in number; no, it increased, it is true, as a person with dropsy increases; it swelled up in unhealthy fat, almost nauseatingly expanded in carnal obesity, scarcely recognizable. (PIC-230)

332. The person who inquires about the probable and only about that in order to adhere to it does not ask what is right and what is wrong, what is good and what is evil, what is true and what is false. No, he asks impartially: which is the probable so that I can believe it—whether it is the true is a matter of indifference or is at least of less importance; which is the probable, so that I can adopt it and side with it—whether it is evil or wrong is a matter of indifference or is at least of less importance, if only it is the probable or something that offers the probability of gaining power. (JFY-104)

333. . . . That Christendom and the world are almost indistinguishable, or all become Christians; Christianity has completely conquered—that is, it is abolished! (JFY-188)

334. To be a Christian—well, if only one does not literally steal, does not literally make stealing one's occupation . . . . To be a Christian—well, if in committing adultery one does not overdo or, forsaking the golden mean, carry it to extremes . . . that is, secretly with good taste and culture, it can still be combined with being an earnest Christian who listens to a sermon at least once for every fourteen times he reads comedies and novels. (JFY-188)

335. The Middle Ages thought Christianity meant renunciation, dying to the world, asceticism. Mynster thinks Christianity is almost the same as culture and education (the modern view, generally). (JFY-256)

336. What does it mean, after all, that all these thousands and thousands as a matter of course call themselves Christians! These many, many people, of whom by far the great majority, according to everything that can be discerned, have their lives in entirely different categories, something one can ascertain by the simplest observation! People who perhaps never once go to church, never think about God, never name his name except when they curse! People to whom it has never occurred that their lives should have some duty to God, people who either maintain that a certain civil impunity is the highest or do not find even this to be entirely necessary! Yet all these people, even those who insist that there is no God, they all are Christian, call themselves Christians, are recognized as Christians by the state, are buried as Christians by the Church, are discharged as Christians to eternity! (POV-41)

337. Every once in a while a pastor makes a little fuss in the pulpit about there being something not quite right with all these many Christians—but all those who hear him and who are present there, consequently all those he is speaking *to*, are Christians, and of course he is not speaking to those he is speaking *about*. This is most appropriately called simulated motion. (POV-42)

338. . . . Most people in Christendom are Christians only in imagination. In what categories do they live? They

live in esthetic or, at most, esthetic-ethical categories.
(POV-43)

339.   If it is true that there actually are so few true Christians
in Christendom, then these are *eo ipso* obliged to be
missionaries, even though a missionary in Christendom
will always look different from a missionary in paganism. (POV-47)

340.   If in a word I were to express my judgment of the age, I
would say: It lacks religious upbringing. To become and
be a Christian has become a banality. The esthetic plainly
has the upper hand. (POV-78)

341.   From the highest Christian point of view, there is no
established Church, only a Church militant. (POV-250)

342.   . . . Bishop Mynster's proclamation of Christianity (to
take just one thing) tones down, veils, suppresses, omits
some of what is most decisively Christian, what is too
inconvenient for us human beings, what would make
our lives strenuous, prevent us from enjoying life—this
about dying to the world, about voluntary renunciation, about hating oneself, about suffering for the doctrine, etc. (M-3)

343.   Truly, there is something that is more against Christianity
and the essence of Christianity than any heresy, any
schism, more against it than all heresies and schisms
together, and it is this: to play at Christianity . . . . It is
playing at Christianity: to remove all the dangers
(Christianly, *witness* and *danger* are equivalent), to re-
place them with power, . . . goods, advantages, abun-
dant enjoyment of even the most select refinements—

and then to play the game that Bishop Mynster was a truth-witness . . . (M-6)

344.   *Truth-witness* relates to Christianity's heterogeneity with this world, from which it follows that *the witness* must always be distinguishable by heterogeneity with this world . . . (M-10)

345.   . . . Mynster's preaching stands in relation to the Christianity of the New Testament as Epicureanism to Stoicism, or as cultivation, improvement, polish stand in relation to fundamental change, radical cure. At no point does his preaching ever lead to the essentially Christian, to what is everywhere in the New Testament, a break, the most profound, the most incurable break with this world. (M-17)

346.   "Bishop Mynster was not really a preacher of repentance." But this, especially for a truth-witness, is malpractice, since all truly Christian preaching is first and foremost the preaching of repentance. (M-18)

347.   . . . I would rather gamble, booze, wench, steal, and murder than take part in making a fool of God, would rather spend my days in the bowling alley, in the billiard parlor, my nights in games of chance or at masquerades than participate in the kinds of earnestness Bishop Martensen calls Christian earnestness. (M-21)

348.   . . . A Christian nation composed of ones who honestly confess that they are not Christian, likewise honestly confess that their lives by no means can be called a striving toward what the New Testament understands by Christianity—a Christian nation such as that is an impossibility. (M-37)

349. Luther, you had 95 theses—terrible! And yet, in a deeper sense, the more theses, the less terrible. The matter is far more terrible—there is only one thesis. The Christianity of the New Testament does not exist at all . . . (M-39)

350. "Grace" cannot possibly stretch so far; one thing it must never be used for—it must never be used to suppress or to diminish the requirement. In that case "grace" turns all Christianity upside down. (M-47)

351. . . . An honest rebellion against Christianity can be made only if one honestly acknowledges what Christianity is and how one relates oneself to it. (M-48)

352. . . . Official Christianity is not the Christianity of the New Testament, resembles it no more than the square resembles the circle, no more than enjoying resembles suffering, than loving oneself resembles hating oneself, than craving the world resembles hating the world, than being completely at home in the world resembles being a stranger and alien in the world, than going shopping, dancing, and courting resemble following Christ—no, no more. (M-52)

353. It is Christ's own words: Will the son of man when he comes again, find faith upon the earth? . . . He does not seem to expect the situation to be such that there would be no one who called himself a Christian. After all, he does not say: Will the Son of man find no Christians? What if he had imagined it to be this way: there will be millions of Christians, Christian states, countries, a Christian world, thousands of pastors carrying on their trade—but faith (what I understand by faith), I wonder, will it be found on the earth? (M-58)

354.   If it was possible to attack a merchant in such a way that one showed that his goods were bad but this still did not have the slightest influence on his customary sales of goods, he would presumably say, "Such an attack is of no importance to me at all, because whether the goods are good or bad does not in itself concern me. After all, I am a merchant, and what concerns me is the sales. Indeed, I am to such a degree a merchant that if it could be shown . . . that what I am selling under the name of coffee is not coffee at all—if only I am assured that this attack has no influence whatever on the sales, such an attack is of no importance to me at all . . ." (M-61)

355.   Indeed a low price is not to be recommended unconditionally, has its limitations; if one does not obtain what one buys at the unprecedented low price—then the price is not low but very high. It is the same with Christianity . . . (M-64)

356.   . . . Nothing is more dangerous for true Christianity, nothing is more against its nature, than getting people light-mindedly to assume the name "Christians," to teach them to have a low opinion of being a Christian, as if it were something that is so very easy. (M-95)

357.   I have in my possession a book that probably is almost unknown here in our country, and therefore I will give the precise title: *The New Testament of our Lord and Savior Jesus Christ.* (M-101)

358.   In "Christendom" . . . what is found is not Christianity but an enormous illusion, and people are not pagans but are made blissfully happy in the delusion that they are Christians. (M-107)

359.   But the eternal is not something like that, indifferent to the way in which it is obtained; no, the eternal really is not a something but is—the way in which it is obtained. . . . It is obtained in only one way, in eternity's hard way, to which Christ points with the words: The way is narrow and the gate is strait that leads to life, and few there are who find it. (M-110)

360.   Consequently to this degree the New Testament is no longer the truth: the way is the broadest, the gate is the widest, and we are all Christians. . . . To the degree to which we are all Christians. . . . To that degree to which we are all Christians, to that degree the New Testament is no longer the truth. (M-115)

361.   On these assumptions, the New Testament, considered as guidance for the Christian, becomes a historical curiosity, somewhat like a handbook for travelers in a particular country when everything in that same country is completely changed. Such a handbook is not to be taken seriously by travelers in that country, but it has great value as entertaining reading. (M-123)

362.   . . . The difference between the atheist and official Christianity is that the atheist is an honest man who directly *teaches* that Christianity is fiction, poetry; official Christianity is a falsification that solemnly assures that Christianity is something else entirely, solemnly declaims against atheism, and by means of this covers up that it is itself *making* Christianity into poetry and abolishing the imitation of Christ . . . (M-129)

363.   . . . If you know nothing else about what Christianity is
        than what you know from the Sunday sermons . . . you
        will never have heard the words from Christ. (M-132)

364.   No, what I could be tempted to propose is the follow-
        ing divine worship service: the congregation is as-
        sembled, a prayer is prayed at the church door, a hymn
        is sung, then the pastor ascends the pulpit, picks up the
        New Testament, pronounces God's name, and then reads
        before the congregation the specified passage loudly and
        clearly—after that he must be silent and remain stand-
        ing silent in the pulpit for five minutes, and then he
        may go. (M-132)

365.   . . . It is playing at Christianity . . . It means to counter-
        feit, to mimic a danger where there is no danger, and in
        such a way that the more art one applies to it the more
        deceptively one can pretend as if there were danger. This
        is the way soldiers play at war on the parade grounds;
        there is no danger, but one pretends as if there were,
        and the art consists of making everything deceptive, just
        as if it were a matter of life and death. (M-133)

366.   What Christianity wants is: imitation. What the human
        being does not want is to suffer, least of all the kind of
        suffering that is authentically Christian, to suffer at the
        hands of people. So he discards imitation and thereby
        suffering, the distinctly Christian suffering. (M-135)

367.   "State" is related directly to number. . . . Christianity is
        related to number in another way: one single true Chris-
        tian is enough for it to be true that Christianity exists.
        (M-143)

368. Christianity has been *abolished* by *propagation*, by these millions of Christians in name only, the number of which presumably is supposed to cover up that there is no Christian, that Christianity does not exist at all. (M-143)

369. If there is some issue important to society, people ordinarily concentrate their energy on having a committee established. Once it is established, they are reassured, do not concern themselves very much about the committee's doing anything, and finally forget the whole thing. (M-147)

370. People think . . . there must also be an oath, an oath that guarantees that it is in earnest and remains in earnest. Thus the taking of the oath is true earnestness— whether it is kept or not is of less concern. (M-147)

371. That a person needs medical help is something so palpably understandable that the state does not need to help people to understand it. But when people are made free religiously, one can have plenty of trouble in making their spiritual need clear to them. (M-151)

372. That a proper diagnosis (the opinion about the illness) is more than half the job, every physician will admit, and likewise that all other competence, all solicitude and care, do not help if the diagnosis is wrong. So also with regard to the religious. (M-157)

373. *Christianity's interest*, what it wants is: true Christians. The clergy's egotism, for the sake of financial advantage as well as of power, is connected with: many Christians. And that is very easily done; there is nothing to it. Get

hold of the children, drop a little water on each child's head—then he is a Christian. If a number of them do not even receive their drops, it makes no difference if they just imagine that they did and along with that, in turn, imagine that they are Christians. Then in a very short time we have more Christians than there are herring in the herring season . . . (M-161)

374. The Christianity of the New Testament, however, is what to the highest degree displeases and shocks people. . . . Rare in any generation is a person who exercises the power over himself to be able to *will* what does not please him, so that he is able to hold firmly to the truth that does not please him . . . (M-170)

375. . . . Then we play the game that we all are Christian, all love God, whereas people today interpret "God is love" and "to love God" as nothing but the syrupy sweets stocked by truth witnesses of the lie. (M-178)

376. That not everyone is a genius is no doubt something everyone will admit. But that a Christian is even more rare than a genius—this has knavishly been totally consigned to oblivion. The difference between a genius and a Christian is that the genius is nature's extraordinary; no human being can make himself into one. A Christian is freedom's extraordinary or, more precisely, freedom's ordinary, except that this is found extraordinarily seldom, is what every one of us should be. (M-180)

377. But let us not be fooled by the circumstance that it is open to all, possible for all, as if from that it followed that it is something rather easy, and that there are many

Christian. No, it must be possible for all; otherwise it would not be freedom's extraordinary; but a Christian still becomes even more rare than a genius. (M-180)

378.   Christianity's idea was: to want to change everything. The result, "Christendom's" Christianity is: that everything, unconditionally everything, has remained as it was, only that everything has taken the name of "Christian." . . . (M-185)

379.   That the human being is a defiant creature is well known, but that he is to a high degree a sagacious creature . . . is not always perceived. When there is something that does not please the human being, he sagaciously looks to see whether the power that is in command is weaker than the opposing power that he can command. If he is convinced of that, the rebellion is made in defiance. But if the power that commands what does not please the human being is so superior to him that he unconditionally despairs of rebelling in defiance—then he resorts to hypocrisy. This is the case with Christianity. That the fall from Christianity happened long ago has not been noticed because the fall happened, the rebellion was carried out—in hypocrisy. Christendom itself is the fall from Christianity. (M-189)

380.   One cannot live on nothing. One hears this so often, especially from pastors. And the pastors are the very ones who perform this feat: Christianity does not exist at all—yet they live on it. (M-204)

381.   No, the most dangerous kind of indifferentism, and the very common kind, is to have a specific religion, but this religion is diluted and botched into sheer blather;

therefore one can have the religion in an entirely passionless way. It is the most dangerous kind of indifferentism, because, simply by having this trumpery under the name of religion, one is, so one thinks, safeguarded against . . . every charge that one has no religion. All religion involves passion, having passion. (M-209)

382. They all are: the public. This humanness, to ask whether an opinion is in itself true, no one cares about; what they care about is: how many have this opinion. (M-209)

383. Imagine that there was a mighty spirit who had promised a few people his protection, but on the condition that they should present themselves at a specific place that involved danger to reach—suppose now that these people failed to appear at this specific place but went around in their living rooms at home and spoke enthusiastically with each other about how the spirit had promised them his powerful protection; hence no one would be able to harm them—is this not ludicrous? (M-214)

384. . . . Certainly about the most ludicrous [thing] it is possible to imagine: that God should let himself be *born*, that *the truth* should have entered into the world—in order to make banal remarks; and likewise a new difficulty, the difficulty of explaining that Christ then could be crucified, inasmuch as in this world of banality the death sentence is ordinarily not passed on the making of banal remarks. (M-221)

385. . . . The church, however, is a theater that in every way dishonestly seeks to conceal what it is. (M-221)

386. God's Word says "First the kingdom of God," and the interpretation, perhaps even "the perfecting" of it (since one does not want to do it shabbily) is: first everything else and *last* the kingdom of God; at long last the things of this earth are obtained *first*, and then finally last of all a sermon about—first seeking God's kingdom. In this way one becomes a pastor . . . (M-235)

387. A boy fifteen years old! If it were a matter of ten rix-dollars, the father would say: No, my boy, you can't be allowed to have that at your disposal; you are too damp behind the ears for that. But when it is a matter of his eternal salvation . . . the age of fifteen years is most appropriate. (M-243)

388. There is an adage that says: It is a poor soldier who does not hope to become a general. . . . So it is also in connection with Christianity. Instead of proclaiming the ideals, only what experience teaches is introduced, what the experience of all the centuries teaches, that millions attain only mediocrity. Then Christianity is introduced: *reassuringly*. (M-313)

389. To assume the truth of Christianity on the basis of trust in this demonstration [the demonstration by pastors] is as meaningless as for a person to regard himself as a man of means because much money that does not belong to him passes through his hands, or because he owns a lot of banknotes issued by a bank that has no assets. (M-325)

390. The kind of people now living are altogether incapable of bearing anything as strong as the Christianity of the New Testament (they would perish as a result of it or

lose their minds), in the very same sense as children cannot tolerate strong drink, which is why a little lemonade is prepared for them—and the official Christianity is lemonade-blather for the kind of creatures that are now called human beings, is the strongest they are able to bear; and in their language they call this blather Christianity, just as children call their lemonade wine. (M-333)

391.   So Christianity taught: renunciation. But, says Christendom, Christianity is perfectible, we hereby cannot stand still. Renunciation is an element; we must go further . . . (M-335)

392.   Christianity is a gift, if you will, stipulated for humanity according to the testament of the Savior of the world. But there is a responsibility . . . the gift and the responsibility correspond to each other altogether equally . . . the responsibility is: the imitation of Jesus Christ. (M-336)

393.   Bishop Mynster's service to Christianity is essentially that, through his outstanding personality, his culture, his superiority in distinguished and most distinguished circles, he has created the fashion or more solemn way of regarding Christianity as something no deep and earnest person (how flattering to the persons concerned) could do without. (M-396)

394.   So it is also with playing at Christianity—it is to simulate the Christian proclamation in such a way that everything, everything, everything is included as convincingly as possible, but one thing is omitted—the dangers. (M-433)

395.   I went to him. I said: I am in complete disagreement with you, in disagreement as much as is possible. . . . Bishop Mynster replied: you are the complement to me. (M-437)

396.   . . . Christianity is truth, and the truth that discloses. (M-448)

397.   Christianity is the unconditioned, and to relate oneself unconditionally to the unconditioned means *eo ipso* that the conditioned is to be sacrificed. (M-451)

398.   If one were to describe this entire orthodox apologetic endeavor in a single sentence, yet also categorically, one would have to say: Its aim is to make *Christianity probable*. Then one must add: If this succeeds, then this endeavor would have the ironical fate that on the very day of victory it would have forfeited everything and completely cashiered Christianity. (BOA-39)

399.   . . . Assert the *improbability* of Christianity. (BOA-40)

400.   To be Christian because one is born of Christian parents is the fundamental illusion from which a host of others is derived. (BOA-135)

Purity of Heart

401.   And yet if unity does not lie at the base of diversity, similarity at the base of dissimilarity, then everything has disintegrated. (EUD-193)

402. . . . The purest of heart is precisely the one most willing to comprehend his own guilt most deeply. . . . Without purity no human being can see God and without becoming a sinner no human being can come to know him. (TDIO-15)

403. So what is sought is given. God is near enough, but no one *without purity* can *see God,* and sin is impurity, *and therefore no one can become aware of God without becoming a sinner.* (TDIO-28)

404. Purity of heart is to will one thing. (UDVS-24)

405. If double-mindedness were to be designated briefly with one single appropriate term, what would be more descriptive than . . . "if" or "in case"! (UDVS-48)

406. . . . It is the good that out of love for the learner has invented the punishment. (UDVS-51)

407. To say that double-mindedness wills the good only to a certain degree is basically the expression for all double-mindedness in its relation to the good. (UDVS-64)

408. . . . In busyness there is double-mindedness. (UDVS-66)

409. So there was a double-mindedness that . . . willed the good *for the sake of reward, out of fear of punishment, or in self-willfulness.* But there was another double-mindedness, the double-mindedness of weakness . . . that wills the good with a kind of sincerity, *but only to a certain degree.* (UDVS-78)

V. The Christian Life on Trial

Temptation and Trial

410. . . . The terrible struggle is with the eternal, with God and with oneself. (EUD-199)

411. The difference between sin and spiritual trial (for the conditions in both can be deceptively similar) is that the temptation to sin is in accord with inclination, [that] of spiritual trial [is] contrary to inclination. (COA-174)

412. In temptation, it is the lower that tempts; in spiritual trial it is the higher. (CUP-459)

413. . . . The most terrible struggle is the struggle over the highest. (UDVS-205)

414. . . . Jesus Christ, who truly learned to know every temptation by holding out in every temptation. (WA-120)

415. To be a human being, to live here in this world, is to be tested. (PIC-183)

416. . . . It is to victory that you call him, but this of course means that you call him to struggle and promise him victory in the struggle. (PIC-201)

417. In this world Christ's Church can truly endure only by struggling . . . (PIC-212)

418. . . . There truly is only one possible rescue for Christianity: rigorousness. It cannot be rescued with the help of leniency . . . (PIC-227)

419.   . . . Wherever God is present progress will be recognizable by mounting demands, by the cause becoming harder. On the other hand, the human way is always recognizable by matters being made easier; and that is called progress. (D-171)

Obedience

420.   . . . Obedience is more precious to God than cosmopolitan, philanthropic, patriotic sacrifices upon the altar of humanity. (SOLW-260)

421.   Humanly viewed, the suffering itself is the first danger, but the second danger, even more terrible, is: failing to learn obedience! (UDVS-255)

422.   And if he does not learn obedience, then he may learn what is most corrupting—learn craven despondency, learn to quench the spirit, learn to deaden any noble fervor in it, learn defiance and despair. (UDVS-256)

423.   But what is all eternal truth except this: that God rules; and what is obedience except this: to let God rule; and what other connection and harmony are possible between the temporal and the eternal than this—that God rules and to let God rule! (UDVS-257)

424.   The story tells of at least three, in fact five, people who walked "along the same road," whereas, spiritually speaking, we have to say that each one walked his own road. . . . The first was a peaceful traveler who walked . . . on a lawful road. The second man was a robber who walked . . . on an unlawful road. Then a priest . . .

went . . . on his usual light-minded road. . . . Next a Levite came . . . walking his way, the way of selfishness and callousness. Finally a Samaritan came "along the same road." He found the poor unfortunate man on the road of mercy he demonstrated by his example how one walks on the road of mercy; he demonstrated that the road, spiritually speaking, is precisely this: how one walks. This is why the Gospel says to the learner, "Go and do likewise." (UDVS-290)

425.   . . . He [the public official] should not be obeyed because he is sagacious, should not be obeyed for this reason or that etc., but because he has authority. . . . Duty is to be done because it ought to be done. (CD-206)

426.   It is said that by learning to obey one learns to rule, but it is even more certain that by being obedient oneself one can teach obedience. (WA-24)

427.   When you obey as the creation obeys, tomorrow does not exist, that unblessed day invented by garrulousness and disobedience. (WA-38)

428.   The pagan and the natural man have the merely human self as their criterion. . . . Scripture always defines sin as disobedience . . . self-willfulness against God . . . (SUD-81)

429.   The calamity of our age in politics, as in religion and as in everything, is disobedience, not being willing to obey. One only deceives oneself and others by wanting to make us think that it is doubt that is to blame for the calamity and the cause of the calamity—no, it is insubordination—

it is not doubt about the truth of the religious but insubordination to the authority of the religious. (BOA-5)

Sin

430. Pelagianism that is characteristic of the Greek Mentality, so that sin becomes ignorance, misunderstanding, and infatuation, and the element of will therein—pride and defiance—is disregarded. (COI-61)

431. . . . To forget guilt is a new sin. (SOLW-452)

432. It is eternally false that guilt becomes something different even if a century passed by; to say anything like that is to confuse the eternal with what the eternal least resembled, with human forgetfulness. (UDVS-18)

433. Sin is man's corruption. Only the rust of sin can consume the soul—or eternally corrupt it. (CD-102)

434. . . . Sin is not a moment but is an eternal falling away from the eternal; therefore it is not one time . . . (CD-102)

435. With regard to sin, a turning around is required . . . (CD-153)

436. Here in God's house there is essentially discourse about a danger that the world does not know, a danger in comparison with which everything the world calls danger is child's play—the danger of sin. . . . What is spoken about first and must be spoken about first is sin, that you are a sinner, that before God you are a sinner, that

in fear and trembling before this thought you are to forget your earthly need. (CD-172)

437. No, here in God's house, what is spoken of is principally the horror . . . the wrong . . . that rebellion . . . when the human race rebelled against God. . . . Therefore the one who flees in here from the horror outside is making a mistake—flees to something still more terrible! (CD-173)

438. . . . There is nothing to which a human being so desperately firmly clings as to his sin. (WA-143)

439. . . . What makes sin so terrible is that it is before God. . . . The error consisted in considering God as some externality and in seeming to assume that only occasionally did one sin against God. But God is not some externality in the sense that a policeman is. Nor does one only occasionally sin before God, for every sin is before God, or, more correctly, what really makes human guilt into sin is that the guilty one has the consciousness of existing before God. (SUD-80)

440. What constituent, then, does Socrates lack for the defining of sin? It is the will, defiance. (SUD-90)

441. . . . Man has to learn what sin is by a revelation from God; sin is not a matter of a person's not having understood what is right but of his being unwilling to understand it, of his not willing what is right. (SUD-93)

442. Therefore, interpreted Christianly, sin has its roots in willing, not in knowing, and this corruption of willing affects the individual's consciousness. (SUD-95)

443. But eternity . . . has only two rubrics, and "Whatever does not proceed from faith is sin"; every unrepented sin is a new sin and every moment that it remains unrepented is also new sin. (SUD-105)

444. In the deepest sense, the state of sin is the sin; the particular sins are not the continuance of sin but the expression for the continuance of sin; in the specific new sin the impetus of sin merely becomes more perceptible to the eye. (SUD-106)

445. . . . He says: "I will never forgive myself." This is supposed to show how much good there is in him, what a deep nature he has. It is a subterfuge. (SUD-111)

446. . . . God sometimes lets the believer stumble and fall in some temptation or other, precisely in order to humble him and thereby to establish him better in the good . . . (SUD-112)

447. On the whole, it is unbelievable what confusion has entered the sphere of religion since the time when "thou shalt" was abolished as the sole regulative aspect of man's relationship to God. (SUD-115)

448. . . . Sin, however common it is to all, does not gather men together in a common idea, into an association, into a partnership ("no more than the multitude of the dead out in the cemetery form some kind of society"): instead, it splits men up into single individuals and holds each individual fast as a sinner. (SUD-120)

449. . . . Sin is a *human being's corruption*. (PIC-61)

450.	Admittance is only through the consciousness of sin; to want to enter by any other road is high treason against Christianity. (PIC-67)

451.	. . . But he draws him to himself along only one way: through the consciousness of sin. (PIC-154)

452.	. . . The mode of the sin is always the mode of the punishment . . . (POV-19)

453.	. . . Spiritually understood, the human being in his natural state is sick, he is in error, in a self-deception. Therefore he craves most of all to be deceived; then he is allowed not only to remain in error but to feel really at home in the self-deception. (M-225)

454.	From God's point of view the worst we say of the wildest sins—that they are devil-inspired—is very likely more true of mediocrity's sensate enjoyment of life, because ideally, this mediocrity is much further from the higher than the greatest sins. (M-459)

455.	The matter is very simple: will you obey or will you not obey; will you in faith submit to his divine authority or will you take offense—or will you perhaps not take sides—be careful, that also is offense. (BOA-34)

Suffering

456.	Sorrow always has in it something more substantial than pain. (E/O I-148)

457. The first doubt with which pain really begins is this: Why is this happening to me; can it not be otherwise? (E/O I-148)

458. By nature, joy wishes to disclose itself; sorrow wishes to conceal itself, indeed, at times even to deceive. (E/O I-169)

459. . . . All your happiness lacks a blessing, for it lacks adversities . . . (E/O II-109)

460. But Job! The moment the Lord took everything away, he did not first say, "The Lord took away," but first of all he said, "The Lord gave." (EUD-115)

461. It is not the case, as human flabbiness might wish, that the highest life is without dangerous suffering, but it is the case that an apostle is never without an explanation, never without authority. (EUD-329)

462. . . . The word of comfort must first of all wound more deeply before it can heal. (EUD-330)

463. The most effective means of escaping spiritual trial is to become spiritless, and the sooner the better. (COA-117)

464. Whereas esthetic existence is essentially enjoyment and ethical existence is essentially struggle and victory, religious existence is suffering and not as a transient element but as a continual accompaniment. (CUP-288)

465. . . . The religious person continually has suffering with him, wants suffering in the same sense as the immediate person wants good fortune, and wants and has suf-

fering even if the misfortune is not present externally . . . (CUP-434)

466.   . . . Religiousness is inwardness, that inwardness is the individual's relation to himself before God, its reflection within himself, and that it is precisely from this that the suffering comes . . . (CUP-436)

467.   Viewed religiously, the point . . . is to comprehend the suffering and remain in it in such a way that reflection is on the suffering and not *away from* the suffering. (CUP-443)

468.   When Scripture says that God dwells in a broken and a contrite heart, this is not an expression for an accidental, transitory, momentary condition (in that case the word "dwells" would be very unsuitable) but rather for the essential meaning of suffering for the relationship with God. (CUP-445)

469.   . . . It is finite impatience that wants to have at cheap, second-hand prices the highest, which is dearly bought at first-hand. (TA-89)

470.   . . . One learns more profoundly and reliably what the highest is by reflecting on sufferings than by reflecting on achievements . . . (UDVS-100)

471.   . . . For many people it seems impossible to unite freedom and suffering in the same thought. (UDVS-117)

472.   It can never occur to the natural man to wish for suffering. . . . And he [Jesus] came into the world—in order to suffer. (UDVS-250)

473.   . . . Through sufferings, by himself in sufferings, a person will with the help of God learn the highest truth . . . (UDVS-251)

474.   What heavy suffering: to have to be the stumbling stone in order to be the Savior of the world! (UDVS-254)

475.   When a person suffers and wills to learn from what he suffers, *he continually comes to know only something about himself and about his relationship to God; this is the sign that he is being educated for eternity.* Alas, it is certainly true that through sufferings a person comes to know a great deal about the world . . . but all this knowledge is not the schooling of sufferings. (UDVS-257)

476.   The school of sufferings educates for eternity. We ordinarily speak in another way about schooling; we say that one school educates for science, another for art, a third for a specific occupation . . . (UDVS-260)

477.   . . . The length of the school period has a direct relation to the significance of what one is to become. . . . The longest school educates for the highest; the school that continues just as long as time can educate only for eternity. (UDVS-260)

478.   . . . Although one ordinarily grows older in going to school, and that is just as it should be, in eternity's school one becomes younger, and that is just as it should be. . . . Eternal life is rejuvenation. (UDVS-261)

479.   . . . The true declaration of honor is this: I suffer at all times as guilty—so certain is it in all eternity that God is love. Alas, in paganism the happiest of all thoughts

was secured only by one's being able to think that one was in the right in relation to God. (UDVS-274)

480. To sit with a sufferer and have nothing to do is even harder than to be one—then it is likewise so that where there is task there is hope. . . . The horror of hopelessness . . . Indeed, when there is nothing to do, when not even the suffering itself is the task, then there *is* hopelessness . . . (UDVS-275)

481. But if before God he is never pure and is always without excuse, then he is always guilty, even when he suffers. But if he always suffers as guilty, then it is eternally certain that God is love, and then there is the joy that there are always tasks, always things to do. (UDVS-279)

482. When does temporal suffering weigh most appallingly on a person? Is it not when it seems to him to have no meaning, procures and acquires nothing; is it not when suffering, as the impatient person expresses it, is meaningless and pointless? (UDVS-313)

483. But when it becomes indefinite how great the suffering actually is, the suffering becomes greater; this indefiniteness increases the suffering immensely. (WA-16)

484. Thus we also extol our age because Christianity is no longer persecuted. I think that it does not exist at all. If it did exist in its truth, persecution would instantly follow . . . (JFY-141)

485. What Christianity wants is: imitation. What the human being does not want is to suffer, least of all the kind of suffering that is authentically Christian, to suffer at the

hands of people. So he discards imitation and thereby suffering, the distinctly Christian suffering. (M-135)

486.   . . . And when God wishes to bind a human being to Him in earnest, He summons one of His most faithful servants, His trustiest messenger, Grief, and tells him: Hurry after him, overtake him, do not budge from his side . . . (D-20)

487.   . . . Being known by God makes life infinitely burdensome. (D-20)

Despair

488.   . . . If a vast, never appeased emptiness hid beneath everything, what would life be then but despair? (FAT-15)

489.   Have you reflected upon what it means to despair? It means to deny that God is love! (UDVS-101)

490.   However the customary view of despair does not go beyond appearances, and thus it is a superficial view, that is, no view at all. It assumes that every man must himself know best whether he is in despair or not. Anyone who says he is in despair is regarded as being in despair, and anyone who thinks he is not is therefore regarded as not. (SUD-22)

491.   . . . Whenever that which triggers his despair occurs, it is immediately apparent that he has been in despair his whole life. (SUD-24)

492. . . . Deep, deep within the most secret hiding place of happiness there dwells also anxiety, which is despair. (SUD-25)

493. . . . Only that person's life was wasted who went on living so deceived by life's joys or its sorrows that he never became decisively and eternally conscious as spirit, as self, or, what amounts to the same thing, never became aware and in the deepest sense never gained the impression that there is a God and that "he," he himself, his self, exists before this God—an infinite benefaction that is never gained except through despair. (SUD-26)

494. The philistine-bourgeois mentality [is] triviality, which also essentially lacks possibility. The philistine-bourgeois mentality is spiritlessness; determinism and fatalism are despair of spirit, but spiritlessness is also despair. (SUD-41)

495. . . . The greater the degree of consciousness, the more intensive the despair . . . The devil's despair is the most intensive . . . his despair is the most absolute defiance. This is despair at its maximum. (SUD-42)

496. . . . The esthetic category of spiritlessness does not provide the criterion for what is and what is not despair; what must be applied is the ethical-religious category . . . (SUD-45)

497. The opposite of being in despair is to have faith or hope. (SUD-49)

498. . . . Despair does not come from the outside but from within. (SUD-99)

499. To sin is: "after being taught by a revelation from God what sin is, before God in despair not to will to be oneself or in despair to will to be oneself . . . (SUD-101)

500. Most men are characterized by a dialectic of indifference and live a life so far from the good (faith) that it is almost too spiritless to be called sin—indeed, almost too spiritless to be called despair. (SUD-101)

501. If the others are going to hell, then I am going along with them. But I do not believe that; on the contrary, I believe that we will all be saved, I, too, and this awakens my deepest wonder. (M-478)

Death

502. Somewhere in England there is a gravestone with only these words on it: The Unhappiest One. I can imagine that someone would read it and think that no one at all lied buried there but that it was destined for him. (E/O I-545)

503. Why has no one returned from the dead? Because life does not know how to captivate as death does, because life does not have the persuasiveness that death has. (R-176)

504. Earnestness is that you think death, and that you are thinking it as your lot, and that you are then doing what death is indeed unable to do—namely that you are and death also is. (TDIO-75)

505.   When death comes the word is: Up to here, not one step further . . . (TDIO 78)

506.   . . . The terse but impelling cry of earnestness, like death's terse cry, is: This very day. (TDIO-83)

507.   Let us eat and drink, because tomorrow we shall die—but this is sensuality's cowardly lust for life, that contemptible order of things where one lives in order to eat and drink instead of eating and drinking in order to live. (TDIO-83)

508.   Death does indeed make all equal, but if this equality is in nothing, in annihilation, then the equality is itself indefinable. (TDIO-85)

509.   Earnestness . . . understands that death makes all equal, and this it has already understood, because earnestness has taught it to seek before God the equality in which all are able to be equal. (TDIO-89)

510.   The equality of death is terrifying because nothing can withstand it (how disconsolate!), but the godly equality is blessed because nothing can prevent it unless the person himself wills to do so. (TDIO-90)

511.   So death is indefinable—the only certainty, and the only thing about which nothing is certain. (TDIO-91)

512.   Finally, it must be said of death's decision that it is *inexplicable.* . . . Death itself explains nothing. (TDIO-96)

513.   . . . Death does not forget itself, he [the sensualist] does not slip past death; it has power over what belongs to

this world and changes to nothing that one and only thing the sensualist wanted. (UDVS-27)

514. . . . This kinship of death, this cannot be disavowed. (WOL-345)

515. The world must hate someone who has died to the world; there is nothing that contemporaries tolerate less in a contemporary than living as one who has died to the world. (CD-147)

516. Christianly understood, there is infinitely much more hope in death than there is in life . . . (SUD-8)

517. To use death as a conclusion is a paralogism . . . (BOA-8)

Dying to self

518. Socrates can be used as an example. He was an intellectual tragic hero. His death sentence is announced to him. At that moment he dies, for anyone who does not understand that it takes the whole power of the spirit to die and that the hero always dies before he dies will not advance very far in his view of life. (FAT-177)

519. But someone dead who awakens to life in a new sphere was and is and remains truly dead. (CUP-447)

520. . . . The relationship with God is distinguishable by the negative, and self-annihilation is the essential form for the relationship with God. (CUP-461)

521.   . . . The Christian lives by dying. (CD-17)

522.   The Christian has no self-will whatever; he surrenders himself unconditionally. (CD-64)

523.   There is only one obstacle for God, a person's selfishness, which comes between him and God like the earth's shadow when it causes the eclipse of the moon. (CD-129)

524.   Thus, also in Christian terminology death is indeed the expression for the state of deepest spiritual wretchedness, and yet the cure is simply to die, to die to the world. (SUD-6)

525.   Therefore, death first; you must first die to every merely earthly hope, to every merely human confidence; you must die to your selfishness, or to the world, because it is only through your selfishness that the world has power over you; if you are dead to your selfishness, you are also dead to the world. (FSE-77)

526.   . . . His selfishness would certainly be very deeply wounded by being deprived of the object, but he perceived quire correctly that his selfishness would be even more deeply wounded if the requirement was that he himself must deprive himself of the object. (FSE-78)

527.   This life-giving spirit is not a *direct* heightening of the natural life in a person in *immediate* continuation from and connection with it—what blasphemy! How horrible to take Christianity in vain this way!—it is a new life. . . . Death goes in between; this is what Christianity

teaches, you must die to. The life-giving Spirit is the very one who slays you; the first thing the life-giving Spirit says is that you must enter into death, that you must die to . . . (FSE-76)

528.   Is it cruel to be, if you please, cruel when it is unconditionally the only thing that can save from ruin and help pull through? (FSE-81)

529.   A true martyr has never used power but has contended by means of powerlessness. He compelled people to become aware. Indeed, God knows, they did become aware—they put him to death. Yet he was willing to have that happen. He did not think that his death halted him in his work; he understood that his death was part of it—that the momentum of his work began precisely with his death. (POV-50)

530.   All religion in which there is any truth, certainly Christianity, aims at a person's total transformation and wants, through renunciation and self-denial, to wrest away from him all that, precisely that, to which he immediately clings, in which he immediately has his life. For that kind of religion, as he understands it, the "human being" has no use. (M-248)

Repentance

531.   But there is also a love with which I love God, and this love has only one expression in language—it is "repentance." If I do not love him in this way, then I do not love him absolutely, out of my innermost being. (E/O II-216)

532.   . . . When the finite spirit would see God, it must begin as guilty. (COA-106)

533.   Sin advances in its consequence; repentance follows it step by step, but always a moment too late. (COA-115)

534.   . . . The more profound he is, the more profound is his repentance. But repentance cannot make him free . . . (COA-116)

535.   But when it is a matter of your own accounting, then you certainly would do wrong to forgive yourself the least little thing, because one's own righteousness is even worse than one's own blackest private guilt. (TDIO-12)

536.   . . . Fear to avoid the Holy One. If a person is to understand his sin essentially, he must understand it because he becomes alone, he alone, just he alone, with the Holy One, who knows everything. Only this fear and trembling is the true fear and trembling . . . (TDIO-27)

537.   . . . The less a person thinks of himself, not as humanity in general or as a human being, but of himself as an individual human being, and not with regard to his talents but with regard to his guilt, the more manifest God becomes to him. (TDIO-29)

538.   All comparison is worldly, all emphasis upon it is a worldly attachment in the service of vanity. Even worse than one's own guilt is one's own righteousness . . . (TDIO-31)

539.   Even in daily life everyone experiences that it is more difficult to stand directly before the person of distinction, directly before his royal majesty, than to move in the crowd . . . (TDIO-31)

540.   . . . The confession of sin is not merely a counting of all the particular sins but is a comprehending before God that sin has a coherence in itself. (TDIO-32)

541.   It is easier to hide in the crowd and to drown one's guilt in that of the human race, easier to hide from oneself than to become open in honesty before God. (TDIO-34)

542.   But without honesty there is no repentance. . . . To repent of a generality without substance is a contradiction. (TDIO-34)

543.   We dare not say of repentance and regret that it has its time, that there is a time to be carefree and a time to be crushed in repentance. . . . But if anyone wants to run away from, to be defiant toward, or to sneak away from regret—alas, which is worse, to say that he failed or—that he succeeded! (UDVS-13)

544.   . . . Repentance and regret belong to the eternal in a human being, and thus every time repentance comprehends the guilt it comprehends that it is in the eleventh hour. . . . And in the eleventh hour one understands life quite differently . . . (UDVS-15)

545.   Repentance, then, must have its time. . . . But it must not have its time in the temporal sense, not belong to a certain period of life. . . . Repentance in the sense of

freedom with the stamp of eternity must have its time, yes, even its time for preparation. . . . The eternal with its "at once" must not become the sudden, which merely confuses temporality; on the contrary, it must be of assistance to temporality throughout life. (UDVS-16)

546. . . . But one cannot *confess* without this unity with oneself. (UDVS-20)

547. . . . The Omniscient One does not find out anything about the person confessing, but instead the person confessing finds out something about himself. (UDVS-22)

548. And an error, as we know, never stops by itself; it only goes more and more astray, so that it becomes increasingly difficult to find the way back to the truth. The way of error is easy to find, but to find the way back is very difficult—as is told in the legend of Mount Venus. (WOL-162)

549. The true preacher of repentance has only one aim, to press hard on you or me, on the single individual, to wound him in such a way that he himself now becomes essentially his own preacher of repentance. (CD-192)

550. Oh, deep within every person there dwells a comfort; it is also in there that the preacher of repentance dwells. (CD-196)

551. Ah, but only the penitent properly understands what it is to pray for rest for the soul, rest in the one and only thought in which there is rest for a penitent, that there is forgiveness; rest in the one and only declaration that

can reassure a penitent, that he is forgiven; rest on the one and only ground that can support a penitent, that atonement has been made. (CD-265)

552. There is one thing that is very rare; true sorrow over one's sin . . . (WA-152)

553. And just as when someone has taken a wrong road and pushes ahead on it, he goes further and further away from the truth, deeper and deeper into error, and it becomes worse and worse . . . (JFY-192)

Forgiveness

554. . . . The view that life essentially consists in dying to can be understood both morally and intellectually. It has been understood morally in Christianity, which did not stop with the purely negative . . . the full-grown God-man arises out of it, created after God . . . (COI-76)

555. Healing and reconciliation take place essentially by means of compassion. (E/O II-384)

556. An official forgiveness between two who do not understand each other is an empty gesture and just as dubious as a contract drawn up in writing between two people, one of whom can neither write nor read handwriting. (SOLW-383)

557. The one who takes away the consciousness of sin and gives the consciousness of forgiveness instead—he indeed takes away the heavy burden and gives the light

one in its place. . . . Forgiveness is also a burden . . . even though a light burden . . . (UDVS-246)

558. Christ did not come into the world in order to make life light in the sense of light-mindedness or to make it heavy in the sense of heavy-mindedness but to lay the light burden upon the believer. (UDVS-246)

559. Forgetting, when God does it in relation to sin, is the opposite of creating, since to create is to bring forth from nothing, and to forget is to take back into nothing. (WOL-296)

560. . . . Remember that woman, that there was no one who condemned her. Christ was present. Precisely because he was present, there was no one who condemned her . . . . It would have been of only little help to her that the Pharisees and Scribes went away; after all, they could come again with their condemnation. But the Savior alone remained with her; therefore there was no one who condemned her. (CD-294)

561. The forgiveness of sins is not a matter of particulars—as if on the whole one were good. . . . No, it is just the opposite—it pertains to one's whole self, which is sinful and corrupts everything as soon as it comes in slightest contact with it. (M-395)

562. The one who in truth has experienced and experiences what it is to believe the forgiveness of one's sins has indeed become another person. Everything is forgotten—but still it is not with him as with the child who, after having received pardon, becomes essentially the

same child again. No, he has become an eternity older, for he has now become spirit. All immediacy and its selfishness, its selfish attachment to the world and to himself, have been lost. Now he is, humanly speaking, old, very old, but eternally he is young. (M-395)

563.   It requires more courage to suffer than to act, more courage to forget than to remember, and perhaps the most wonderful thing about God is that he can forget man's sins. *Journal* 1841 (KA-13)

Prayer

564.   Even if an angel spoke with the tongue of an angel in order to describe the beneficial effect of prayer, it would not help the sensate person, because he neither understands nor cares about that for which prayer is beneficial. (EUD-381)

565.   Even if prayer does not accomplish anything here on earth, it nevertheless works in heaven. (EUD-442)

566.   When the Pharisee in the Gospel is portrayed as a hypocrite, this is true only insofar as he feels himself superior to other people, but the rest of what he says is comic as soon as one gives it any thought. . . . The Pharisee thinks he is speaking with God, whereas from what he says it is clear and distinct enough that he is speaking with himself or with another Pharisee. (SOLW-238)

567.   . . . Purity of heart is precisely the wisdom that is gained by praying . . . (UDVS-26)

Pride

568. The proud person always wants to do the right thing, the great thing, and he is actually struggling not with people but with God, because he wants to do it with his own power; he does not want to sneak out of something—no, what he wants is to set the task as high as possible and then to finish it by himself, satisfied with his own consciousness and his own approval. (EUD-354)

569. . . . Then they band together and are proud in a solidarity that is vanity and cowardliness. (EUD-355)

570. What wonder is it, after all, that the significant is significant? But to make the intrinsically insignificant more significant than the most significant—that surely is still a task. (P-28)

571. The devotional work is also Christian, which stands to reason since it addresses itself to the cultured, since the cultured are, of course, Christians. (P-33)

572. A sufferer usually has one or several ways in which he might want to be helped. If he is helped in these ways, then he is glad to be helped. . . . There is the humiliation of being obliged to accept any kind of help unconditionally, of becoming a nothing in the hand of the "Helper" for whom all things are possible, or the humiliation of simply having to yield to another person, of giving up being himself as long as he is seeking help. (SUD-71)

573. Demonic despair is the most intensive form of the despair; in despair to will to be oneself. (SUD-73)

VI. The Christian Life of Faith

Passion

574. Let others complain that the times are evil. I complain that they are wretched, for they are without passion. (E/O I-27)

575. The power cowardliness prefers to conspire with is time, because neither time nor cowardliness finds that there is any reason to hurry. (EUD-356)

576. Cowardliness calmly goes on with its striving and can see very well that week by week, yes, day by day, it is not striving in vain, and neither is it striving toward an infinitely far-off goal. (EUD-358)

577. . . . Cowardliness, you see, has won sagacity over to its side, and sagacity declares that this is absolutely right, because the person who begins nothing does not lose anything either. (EUD-359)

578. . . . Shakespeare knows how to speak the language of passion fluently, a language that in the eminent sense then has the characteristic that if a person cannot speak it fluently he cannot speak it at all—that is, it simply does not exist for him. (SOLW-221)

579. . . . The lostness of spiritlessness is the most terrible of all. (COA-94)

580. The ludicrous aspect of the Zealot was that infinite passion thrust itself upon a wrong object (an approxima-

tion-object), but the good aspect of him was that he did have passion. (CUP-35)

581.   This much is certain: although I am generally not un-acquainted with the comforts of life, of all comforts indolence is the most comfortable. (CUP-186)

582.   . . . For the existing person, passion is existence at its very highest . . . (CUP-197)

583.   It is ordinarily the case that passion and reflection exclude each other. (CUP-611)

584.   If the essential passion is taken away, the one motivation, and everything becomes meaningless externality, devoid of character, then the spring of ideality stops flowing and life together becomes stagnant water—this is crudeness. (TA-62)

585.   Generally speaking, compared to a passionate age, a reflective age devoid of passion *gains in extensity what it loses in intensity.* (TA-97)

586.   Indeed, does [uncontrolled] passion ever really know what it is doing . . . continued in a person it changes his life into nothing but moments, because it perfidiously serves its blinded master while working its way up to making him [the master] serve like a blinded slave! (UDVS-23)

587.   There is one thing of which the lily and the bird know unconditionally nothing—something the majority of human beings, alas, know best—half-measures. (WA-23)

588. And over the years, an individual may abandon the little bit of passion, feeling, imagination, the little bit of inwardness he had and embrace as a matter of course an understanding of life in terms of trivialities . . . (SUD-59)

589. . . . For the majority are eager to be along when it is a matter of nothing more than celebrating and riding in the parade. (PIC-107)

590. It is so easy to trip the light fantastic of desire, but when after a while, it is desire that dances with the person against his will—that is a ponderous dance! . . . Until the passions, having taken the reins given them, tear him along at an even more daring speed . . . (FSE-66)

Choice/Decision/Will

591. The choice itself is crucial for the content of the personality: through the choice the personality submerges itself in that which is being chosen, and when it does not choose, it withers away in atrophy. (E/O II-163)

592. . . . There eventually comes a moment where it is no longer a matter of an Either/Or, not because he has chosen, but because he has refrained from it . . . (E/O II-164)

593. In the world of the spirit, the only one who is shut out is the one who shuts himself out; in the world of the spirit, all are invited. (EUD-335)

594. . . . It is most shocking that someone can know everything and not have made a beginning on the least thing. (TDIO-22)

595. It is my conviction that the will is of primary importance even in connection with thinking, that talents ten
times as good without an energetic will do not consti-
tute as good a thinker as talents ten times as poor combined with an energetic will . . . (SOLW-259)

596. . . . Every beginning, when it is *made* . . . does not occur
by virtue of immanental thinking but *is made* by virtue
of a resolution, essentially by virtue of faith. (CUP-189)

597. By means of the tour de force of not thinking anything
decisive about what is most decisive . . . (CUP-217)

598. . . . The only possible understanding of the absolute
paradox is that it cannot be understood. (CUP-218)

599. What does it mean to assert that a decision is to a certain degree? It means to deny decision. (CUP-221)

600. Now, if to him an eternal happiness is his highest good,
this means that in his acting the finite elements are once
and for all reduced to what must be surrendered in relation to the eternal happiness. (CUP-391)

601. If it does not *absolutely* transform his existence for him,
then he is not relating himself to an eternal happiness;
if there is something he is not willing to give up for its
sake, then he is not relating himself to an eternal happiness. (CUP-393)

602. All relative willing is distinguished by willing something
for something else, but the highest *telos* must be willed
for its own sake. (CUP-394)

603. . . . The specific sign that one relates oneself to the absolute is that not only is there no reward to expect but suffering to endure. (CUP-402)

604. . . . Over the temple at Delphi there was also the inscription: *ne quid nimis* (nothing too much). This motto is the *summa summarum* of all finite worldly wisdom. . . . That maxim, *ne quid nimis*, may be valid in many life relationships, but applied to the absolute passionate relationship, to the absolute *telos*, it is nonsense. On the contrary, the point is absolutely to venture everything, absolutely to stake everything, absolutely to desire the highest *telos*. (CUP-404)

605. On the whole, it is incredible how cunning and inventive people are in avoiding the final decision . . . (CUP-423)

606. The appointed task is simultaneously to relate oneself absolutely to the absolute *telos* and relatively to relative ends. (CUP-431)

607. The highest His Imperial Highness is able to do, however, is to make his decision before God. The accent is upon this: "before God"; the many millions are only an illusion. But the lowliest human being can also make his decision before God, and he who actually was a religious person of such a kind that he could decide before God to go out to the amusement park will not be put to shame alongside any imperial highness. (CUP-497)

608. If it is to be possible for a person to be able to will one thing, he must will the good. (UDVS-24)

609.   . . . The good is unconditionally the one and only thing that a person may will and shall will, and is only one thing. (UDVS-25)

610.   . . . Ah, it is still true that the slightest bread of charity in the service of the good is infinitely more blessed than to be the most powerful one outside it. (UDVS-83)

611.   Making satisfaction is indeed God's plan from eternity. (UDVS-259)

612.   A knowledge that God is love is still not a consciousness of it. Consciousness, personal consciousness, requires that in my knowledge I also have knowledge of myself and my relation to my knowledge. (CD-194)

613.   When did you become a believer or, it amounts to the same thing, are you essentially conscious that you have experienced this decision to become a believer? (CD-217)

614.   The two lovers are so close to each other that as long as the other is alive the one cannot be devoted to someone else without despising the other; therein lies what there is of an either/or in this relationship. (WA-23)

615.   Wherever there is ambivalence, there is temptation. . . . But where there is ambivalence, there is in one way or another also disobedience underneath at the base. (WA-32)

616.   These two powers are so inimical that the slightest leaning to one side is regarded from the other side as the

unconditional opposite. . . . When a human being forgets that he is in this enormous danger, when he thinks that he is not in danger, when he even says peace and no danger—then the Gospel's message must seem to him a foolish exaggeration. (WA-33)

617.	Only in the choice is the heart disclosed. . . . [It is by choice that the heart is revealed.] (PIC-96)

618.	But a self can truly draw another self to itself only through a choice . . . (PIC-159)

619.	And just as it is so that however tenderly the actor and actress embrace and caress each other on the stage, it still always remains only a theatrical connivance, a theater-marriage—in the same way everything "to a certain degree" is theatrical in relation to the unconditional, grasps a delusion; only Either/Or is the embrace that grasps the unconditional. . . . The mark of what is God's service is: Either/Or. (M-94)

Wisdom

620.	. . . To be able to die well is indeed the highest wisdom of life. (TDIO-76)

621.	. . . A man of prayer does not pore over scholarly books but is the wise man "whose eyes are opened—when he kneels down." (Numbers 24: 16) (UDVS-26)

622.	If the fear of the Lord is the beginning of wisdom, then learning obedience is the consummation of wisdom . . . (UDVS-258)

623.   What the world actually admires as sagacity [cunning]
       is knowledge of evil—whereas wisdom is knowledge of
       the good. (WOL-284)

624.   There is, namely, one resistance to the power of the
       years—it is perfectibility, and it is precisely over the years
       that it develops. (CD-324)

625.   The fact or the facts are basic, but the explanation is the
       decisive factor. (WOL-291)

Justice and Judgment

626.   . . . More ashamed before human beings and their
       judgment than before the god and his judgment . . .
       (CUP-183)

627.   Alas, Many think that judgment is something reserved
       for the far side of the grave, and so it is also, but they
       forget that judgment is much closer than that, that it is
       taking place at all times . . . (WOL-227)

628.   But sometimes a change intrudes, a revolution, a war,
       an earthquake, or some such terrible misfortune, and
       everything is confused. Justice tries in vain to secure
       for each person his own; it cannot maintain the distinc-
       tion between *mine* and *yours*; in the confusion it cannot
       keep the balance and therefore throws away the scales—
       it despairs! (WOL-265)

629.   But the crowd can rarely account for its judgment, has
       one opinion today; another tomorrow. (PIC-42)

The Future

630.   Trouble and today correspond to each other; self-torment and the next day also go together. (CD-71)

631.   All earthly and worldly care is basically for the next day. (CD-71)

632.   If there is no next day for you, then either you are dying or you are one who by dying to temporality grasped the eternal, either one who is actually dying or one who is *really* living. (CD-72)

633.   At times we lament and find it sad that the future lies so dark before us. Ah, the misfortune is precisely when it is not dark enough, when fear and presentiment and expectancy and earthly impatience catch a glimpse of the next day! (CD-73)

634.   To be totally contemporary with oneself today with the help of the eternal is also the most formative and generative; it is the gaining of eternity. (CD-74)

635.   The Christian prays, "Save me from evil today." This is the surest deliverance from the next day, but it is also intended to be prayed every day; if it is forgotten one day, the next day promptly makes its appearance. (CD-75)

636.   "Let us eat and drink, because tomorrow we shall die." . . . This very remark echoes with the anxiety about the next day . . . (CD-77)

637.   What is anxiety? It is the next day. (CD-78)

638.   . . . In order to live until tomorrow one must be living today. (CD-79)

Hope

639.   There is a hope that should be killed, just as there is a lust, a craving, and a longing that should be killed— the earthly hope should be killed. (UDVS-116)

640.   When the God-forsaken worldliness of earthly life shuts itself in with itself in complacency, the confined air develops poison in itself and by itself. (WOL-246)

641.   Hope is not implicit in possibility as a matter of course, because in possibility there can also be fear. (WOL-253)

642.   When all misfortunes befell the human race, hope still remained. In this paganism and Christianity agree; the difference is this, and it is an infinite one, that Christianity has an infinitely smaller conception of all these misfortunes and an infinitely more blessed conception of hope. (WOL-259)

643.   Christianly understood, there is infinitely much more hope in death than there is in life . . . (SUD-8)

644.   . . . Where indeed does paganism show its hopelessness more than in its theory of luck! (BOA-291)

Doubt

645.   . . . When I, despite every effort, was unable to ascend to the dizzying thought of doubting everything, I decided, in order nevertheless to doubt something, to concentrate my soul on the more human task of doubting whether all the philosophizers understood what they said and what was said. (P-49)

646.   My purpose, then, is to serve philosophy; my qualification for this is that I am obtuse enough not to understand it, indeed still more obtuse—obtuse enough to betray that. (P-51)

647.   Hegelian philosophy has now thrived for several years here at home. If this philosophy, after having explained everything, now advances and explains itself, what a splendid prospect. . . . I do not deny that Hegel has explained everything. . . . keep my feet on the ground and say: I have not understood Hegel's explanation. . . . keep my feet on the ground; I modulate into another key. I plead, I plead for an explanation, an explanation, note well, that I can understand, because it would scarcely help me if there were to be an explanation that explains everything in Hegel, but in such a way that I cannot understand it. Give me the explanation; I will take it *à tout prix* [at any price]. (P-56)

648.   I am so obtuse that philosophy cannot become understandable to me. The opposite of this is that philosophy is so sagacious that it cannot comprehend my obtuseness. These opposites are mediated into a higher unity, that is, a common obtuseness. (P-58)

649. He [the indecisive person] wants to begin with doubt, precisely this . . . is the insubordination, because in this way God is thrust down from the throne, from being the master. When one has done that, one actually has already chosen another master, self-will, and then becomes the slave of indecisiveness. (CD-88)

VII. The Basis of the Christian Life

Historical Evidence for Christianity

650. . . . Knowing a historical fact—indeed, knowing all the historical facts with the trustworthiness of an eyewitness—by no means makes the eyewitness a follower . . . (PF-59)

651. . . . For the essence of the Socratic is that the learner, because he himself is the truth and has the condition, can thrust the teacher away. . . . Faith, then, must constantly cling firmly to the teacher. (PF-62)

652. In relation to an eternal truth that is supposed to be decisive for an eternal happiness, eighteen centuries have no greater demonstrative weight than a single day. (CUP-47)

653. How can something historical be decisive for an eternal happiness? (CUP-94)

654. If someone wanted to be his follower, his approach, as seen in the Gospel, was different from lecturing. To such a person he said something like this: Venture a decisive

act; then we can begin. . . . The proof does not precede but follows . . . (JFY-191)

Salvation

655.   I can still save my soul as long as my concern that my love of God conquer within me is greater than my concern that I achieve earthly happiness. (FAT-49)

656.   . . . No one has ever, in the sense of the moment, accomplished as little by a life solely committed to sacrifice as did Jesus Christ. Yet, in the eternal sense, at that same moment he had accomplished everything . . . (UDVS-91)

657.   Oh, there is indeed only one friend, one trustworthy friend in heaven and on earth, our Lord Jesus Christ . . . . No friend has ever been able to be more than faithful *unto* death, but he remained faithful *in* death—his death was indeed my salvation. (CD-158)

658.   No, apprehensive about myself as I have become, I will seek my refuge with him, the Crucified One. I will beseech him to save me from evil and to save me from myself. Only when saved by him and with him, only when he holds me fast, do I know that I will not betray him. (CD-280)

659.   . . . If he covered your sin with his life, then there indeed would be the possibility of the danger that they would deprive him of life and you of your hiding place. It is different when he covers your sin with his death. (WA-186)

660.   Here is the dialectic: he wants to save the world by his death; otherwise he cannot save it—but for all that he is not himself responsible for being persecuted and put to death. (WA-209)

661.   What is decisive is that with God everything is possible. . . . At this point, then, salvation is, humanly speaking, utterly impossible; but for God everything is possible! (SUD-38)

662.   Christianity is just as gentle as it is rigorous, just as gentle, that is, infinitely gentle. (POV-16)

663.   Christianity has of course known very well what it wanted. It wants to be proclaimed by *witnesses*—that is, by persons who proclaim the teaching and also existentially express it. (POV-217)

664.   One thing, however, remains—we are still all saved by grace. (POV-220)

665.   Luther is completely right in saying that if a human being had to acquire his salvation by his own striving, it would end either in presumption or in despair, and therefore it is faith that saves. (M-408)

Christian Commitment—the Leap

666.   Resolution is a waking up to the eternal . . . (EUD-347)

667.   . . . It is also wretched to have an abundance of intentions and a poverty of action, to be rich in truths and poor in virtues. (EUD-350)

668.   If making a resolution is understood in this way to be the constant renewal of a crucial resolution . . . then it remains fixed that resolution is a saving means. (EUD-352)

669.   . . . Belief is not a knowledge but an act of freedom, an expression of will. (PF-83)

670.   But one human being cannot teach another true wonder and true fear. Only when they compress and expand your soul—yours, yes yours, yours alone in the whole world, because you have become alone with the Omnipresent One—only then are they in truth for you. (TDIO-25)

671.   If, then, a man who had been regularly listening to a speaker discoursing on religious matters were to go to him and say, "Now that I have listened to you so regularly, do you not think that I now have faith?" (SOLW-444)

672.   . . . The issue is not about the truth of Christianity but about the individual's relation to Christianity. (CUP-15)

673.   God, however, can never become a third party when he is a part of the religion; this is precisely the secret of the religious. (CUP-66)

674.   . . . To have been very close to making the leap is nothing whatever, precisely because the leap is the category of decision. (CUP-99)

675. . . . Decision is the little magic word that existence respects. If, however, the individual refuses to act, existence cannot help. To be like that King Agrippa, not far from believing or acting, is the most enervating state imaginable if one remains in it very long. (TA-66)

676. Not even a suicide these days does away with himself in desperation but deliberates on this step so long and so sensibly that he is strangled by calculation, making it a moot point whether or not he can really be called a suicide, inasmuch as it was in fact the deliberating that took his life. (TA-68)

677. . . . Letting matters reach a verdict and decision without ever acting. (TA-69)

678. They must make the leap themselves, and God's infinite love will not become a second-hand relationship for them. (TA-108)

679. . . . God is present in the moment of choice, not in order to watch but in order to be chosen. (UDVS-207)

680. If you want to show that it is intended for God, then give it away, but with the thought of God . . . . God does not ask for anything for himself, although he asks for everything from you. (WOL-161)

681. Alas, the world thinks very little or never of God; that is why it must misunderstand any life whose most essential and constant thought is the thought of God. . . . But since the world actually does not know and presumably does not want to know of the existence of this criterion (the God-relationship), it cannot explain

such a person's behavior except as an eccentricity. (WOL-202)

682.   Yet this is the highest thing that can be said of any human being: one is sacrificed. The only question is whether it is the highest for which one is sacrificed. (WOL-311)

683.   Every human being at some time, at the beginning, stands at the crossroads—this is his perfection and not his merit. Where he stands at the end (at the end it is not possible to stand at the crossroads) is his choice and his responsibility. (CD-20)

684.   . . . He [Peter] is not a Job who says," The Lord took." No, the apostle uses another expression; he says, we have left everything. (CD-178)

685.   But Christianity is indeed the religion of freedom, and precisely the voluntary is essentially Christian. Voluntarily to give up everything to follow Christ . . . (CD-179)

686.   There is something that God cannot take away from a human being, namely, the voluntary, and it is precisely this that Christianity requires. (CD-179)

687.   Voluntarily to leave everything in order to follow Christ, which the world neither wants nor is able to hear without being offended, is also that which so-called Christendom prefers to have suppressed or, if it is said, would very much like to ignore, or in any case hears in such a way that something different comes out of it. (CD-179)

688. . . . *He* [Peter] *left the certain and chose the uncertain.* Christ, in imitation of whom he left everything, was . . . the poorest of all, he who as far as his own life was concerned was sure of only one thing: that he would be sacrificed. (CD-182)

689. Oh, how rarely is there a person, to say nothing of a generation, that does not indulge in the fraud of habit . . . (CD-314)

690. Of all sophists, time is the most dangerous, and of all dangerous sophists, habit is the most cunning. It is already difficult enough to realize that one changes little by little over the years, but the fraud of habit is that one is the same, unchanged, that one says the same thing, unchanged, and yet is very changed and yet says it, very changed. (CD-315)

691. If I have ventured wrongly, well, then life helps me by punishing me. But if I have not ventured at all, who helps me then? (SUD-34)

692. No one comes to me by way of demonstrations; pay attention to them so that you may become aware— and then, yes, blessed is he who is not offended at me. (PIC-97)

693. . . . And the thoughts of your heart are disclosed as you choose whether you will believe or not. (PIC-136)

694. But a self can truly draw another self to itself only through a choice . . . (PIC-159)

695. . . . The choice is Christ . . . (PIC-160)

696.   . . . The person who never relinquished probability never became involved with God. All religious, to say nothing of Christian, venturing is on the other side of probability, is by way of relinquishing probability. (JFY-99)

697.   To connect God's name with one's wishes, craving, and plans is easy, far too easy for the lightweight; but it does not follow that their venturing is in reliance upon God. (JFY-100)

698.   The person who inquires about the probable and only about that in order to adhere to it does not ask what is right and what is wrong, what is good and what is evil, what is true and what is false. No, he asks impartially: which is the probable so that I can believe it—whether it is the true is a matter of indifference or is at least of less importance; which is the probable, so that I can adopt it and side with it—whether it is evil or wrong is a matter of indifference or is at least of less importance, if only it is the probable or something that offers the probability of gaining power. (JFY-104)

699.   Likewise there are also a few who directly confess that their lives express only this "to a certain degree," and thus their Christianity is not truly Christianity. (JFY-109)

700.   But to sell Christianity as comfort in this way without life commitment—this is indulgence, is doing business with Christianity. (JFY-132)

701.   Christianly, one does not proceed from the simple in order then to become interesting, witty, profound, a poet, a philosopher, etc. No, it is just the opposite; *here* one

begins and then becomes more and more simple, arrives at the simple. (POV-7)

702.   No, only when the man is there, and when he ventures as it must be ventured—then is the moment. . . . But when the right man comes, yes, then is the moment. (M-338)

703.   And yet contemporaneity with what is unshakably the essentially Christian is decisive. (BOA-43)

704.   . . . The Highest, after all, is not to *comprehend* the Highest, but to do it. (D-146)

705.   May 19, 1838 *Half-past ten in the morning.* There is *an indescribable joy* which glows through us as unaccountably as the Apostle's outburst is unexpected: "Rejoice, and again I say, Rejoice." . . . "I rejoice over my joy, in, by, at, on, through, of and with my joy." [Kierkegaard's conversion experience at age 25 recorded in his *Journal* May 19, 1838] (KA-10)

706.   25 Years Old . . . Then it was that the great earthquake occurred, the terrible revolution which suddenly forced upon me a new and infallible law of interpretation of all the facts. *Journal* 1838 (KA-11)

Denial

707.   To desert one's post, to flee in battle, is always dishonorable, but then sagacity [cunning] has come up with an ingenious turn that obligingly forestalls flight—it is evasion. Therefore, through evasion one never gets into

danger and as a result does not lose one's honor by fleeing in danger. (UDVS-82)

708.   Alas, which kind of denial [denial at threat of danger or denial by clever avoidance] is worse? Certainly the latter, the cowardly, ingeniously calculated, daily denial of Christ, continued year after year, dragging on through a whole lifetime incessantly, daily. . . . But there is no salvation for this cunning fame of [cunning]: the secret consists simply in maintaining the appearance that one has not, after all, denied Christ. (CD-180)

709.   "To sin is human, but to continue in sin is diabolical." Yet what we are talking about is even more terrible, this ingenious and conscious adapting of life to sin, or if not with full consciousness of it, at least with the consciousness that one is maintaining an unclarity in one's soul about something that one for good reasons does not wish to clarify. (CD-180)

710.   In God's eyes, therefore, there is no sin as loathsome as the sin of sagacity [cunning], simply because this has the world's approval. . . . The sin of sagacity is to sin in such a way that one ingeniously knows how to avoid punishment, yes, ingeniously knows how to give the appearance of the good. The sin of sagacity is ingeniously to avoid every decision and in that way to win the distinction of never having denied—this the world regards as something extraordinary. (CD-181)

VIII. The Inner Life

The Christian life

711.   An earnest Christian, for example, is well aware that there are moments when he is more profoundly and vitally gripped by the Christian life than he usually is, but he does not therefore become a pagan when the mood passes. (COI-284)

712.   Thus it is proper to say that every duty is essentially duty to God . . . (FAT-68)

713.   The person who is without God in the world soon becomes bored with himself—and expresses this haughtily by being bored with all life, but the person who is in fellowship with God indeed lives with the one whose presence gives infinite significance to even the most insignificant. (TDIO-78)

714.   To know a creed by rote is paganism, because Christianity is inwardness. (CUP-224)

715.   The matter has been turned in such a way that one takes an interest in being a Christian in order to be able to decide what Christianity is, and not in what Christianity is in order to be a Christian. (CUP-612)

716.   I hate habitual Christianity in whatever form it appears. (CA-52)

717.   . . . I have from the beginning understood Christianity to be inwardness and my task to be the inward deepening of Christianity. (CA-53)

718. No, the essentially Christian is certainly the highest and the supremely highest, but, mark well, in such a way that to the natural man it is an offense. (WOL-58)

719. But if you think that you will come closer to this highest with the help of "culture," you make a great mistake. (WOL-59)

720. Therefore the one who truly loves the neighbor loves also his enemy. (WOL-67)

721. Worldly similarity, if it were possible, is not Christian equality. (WOL-72)

722. But if your ultimate and highest goal is to have life made easy and sociable, then never become involved with Christianity, shun it, because it wants the very opposite; it wants to make your life difficult and to do this by making you alone before God. (WOL-124)

723. Christianity is not infrequently presented in a certain sentimental, almost soft, form of love. It is all love and love; spare yourself and your flesh and blood; have good days or happy days without self-concern, because God is Love and Love—nothing at all about rigorousness must be heard; it must all be the free language and nature of love. Understood in this way, however, God's love easily becomes a fabulous and childish conception, the figure of Christ too mild and sickly-sweet for it to be true that he was and is an offense to the Jews, foolishness to the Greeks—that is, as if Christianity were in its dotage. (WOL-376)

724. And how often a victory has been made empty when the victor became proud, conceited, arrogant, and self-satisfied and lost by having conquered! . . . In the spiritual sense, there are always two victories, a first victory and then the second one in which the first victory is preserved! (WOL-332)

725. Only when a person in the very moment of victory relinquishes the victory to God, only then does a person continue to stand . . . (WOL-333)

726. . . . If one is a Christian, one must have become that. (CD-41)

727. What then is the eminent Christian? Well, if you ask in a worldly way whether he is a king or an emperor or his lordship or his grace, etc., it is, of course, generally an impossibility to answer. But if you ask in the Christian sense, the answer is easy: He is a Christian. (CD-50)

728. One can become and be a Christian only as or in the capacity of a lowly person. (CD-53)

729. Christianity has never taught that literally to be a lowly person is synonymous with being a Christian, nor that there is a direct and inevitable transition from literally being a lowly person to becoming a Christian; neither has it taught that if the worldly eminent person relinquished all his power he therefore was a Christian. But from literal lowliness to becoming a Christian there is still only one course. Literally to be a lowly person is no unfortunate introduction to becoming a Christian; to be in the possession of external advantages is a detour that makes a double introduction necessary . . . (CD-54)

730. It is not with him [Christ] as with a human being, who may very well have a friend and an adherent without knowing it, without knowing him; but the one Christ does not know is not his own, because Christ is all-knowing.—He knows them and he knows each one individually. (CD-272)

731. There are also those he does not know, those to whom he will say: "I do not know you, I never knew you." (CD-272)

732. . . . The real reason that men are offended by Christianity is that it is too high, because its goal is not man's goal, because it wants to make man into something so extraordinary that he cannot grasp the thought. (SUD-83)

733. No teaching on earth has ever really brought God and man so close together as Christianity, nor can any do so, for only God himself can do that, and any human fabrication remains just a dream, a precarious delusion. (SUD-117)

734. Christianity did not come into the world as a showpiece of gentle comfort, as the preacher blubberingly and falsely introduces it—but as the absolute. (PIC-62)

735. In relation to the absolute, there is only one time, the present; for the person who is not contemporary with the absolute, it does not exist at all. (PIC-63)

736. This, indeed, was Christianity, not that a rich man makes the poor rich but that the poorest of all makes all rich, both the rich and the poor. (PIC-153)

737.   . . . His [Christ's] life is the prototype. (PIC-202)

738.   But from the Christian point of view, there are two kinds of disorder. The one is tumult, disturbance in externals. The other disorder is the stillness of death, a dying out, and this is perhaps the more dangerous. (FSE-20)

739.   That which distinguishes the Christian narrow way from the common human narrow way is the voluntary. (FSE-67)

740.   . . . As if it would follow naturally that if we only understand the right it follows automatically that we do it. What a grievous misunderstanding or what a sly fabrication! (JFY-116)

741.   According to Christianity, then, the only person who is completely sober is the person whose understanding is action. And so it ought to be. Your understanding must *immediately* be action. Immediately! (JFY-120)

742.   They have changed Christianity and have made it too much of a *consolation,* and forgotten that it is a *demand* upon man. (D-147)

743.   . . . As a rule, Christianity is taught in a merely trivial way . . . (D-156)

744.   *Quarrelling with people about what Christianity is* a mistake, for with very few exceptions their tactics aim at warding off understanding or learning what Christianity is, because they suspect that it is rather easy to grasp, but also that it would interfere with their lives. (D-166)

The Imitation of Christ

745. To follow, then, means to walk along the same road walked by the one whom one is following; it means, therefore, that he is no longer visibly walking ahead. (UDVS-219)

746. And when the child learns to walk by itself, what must the mother do then? She must make herself invisible. That her tenderness remains the same, remains unchanged, yes, that it probably increases at the very time the child is learning how to walk by itself—of this we are well aware. Perhaps, however, the child may not always be able to understand it. . . . To follow, then, means to walk by oneself and to walk alone along the road that the teacher walked—to have no visible person with whom one can take counsel, to have to choose by oneself, to scream in vain . . . (UDVS-220)

747. . . . There is indeed but one name in heaven and on earth, only one single name, and therefore just one road to choose . . . (UDVS-225)

748. Christ went ahead, and not only that, he went ahead in order to prepare a place for the follower. (UDVS-227)

749. Between heaven and earth there is only one road: to follow Christ. (UDVS-229)

750. . . . The road is: *how* it is walked. We cannot indicate the road of virtue and say: *There* runs the road of virtue. We can only say how the road of virtue is walked. (UDVS-289)

751.   Doubt wants to trick the sufferer into thinking about whether it would not still be possible that the hardship could be taken away and he could still continue walking along the same road—without hardship. . . . Doubt wants to trick him into thinking about whether it would not still be possible to take another road. (UDVS-296)

752.   Spiritually, however, the road is: how it is walked, and thus it would surely be odd if on the road of hardship there were the difference that some walked on the road of hardship without hardships. (UDVS-298)

753.   But if hardship is the road, then this road is indeed unconditionally passable. Hardship must lead to something. The road of hardship is the only road where there is no obstacle, because instead of blocking off the road the hardship itself prepares the road. (UDVS-302)

754.   . . . For truly to be a Christian certainly does not mean to be Christ (what blasphemy!) but means to be his imitator, yet not a kind of prinked-up, nice looking successor who makes use of the firm and leaves Christ's having suffered many centuries in the past; no, to be an imitator means that your life has as much similarity to his as is possible for a human life to have. (PIC-106)

755.   . . . Every generation must begin from the beginning with Christ and then set forth his life as the paradigm . . . (PIC-107)

756.   . . . Each individual in it, who in order to travel the way must begin at the very same place, from the beginning, the beginning of the way. (PIC-209)

757.   . . . Rescue us from this error of wanting to admire or adoringly admire you instead of wanting to follow you and be like you. (PIC-233)

758.   He never says that he asks for admirers, adoring admirers, adherents: and when he uses the expression "follower" he always explains it in such a way that one perceives the "imitators" is meant by it . . . (PIC-237)

759.   Christ came to the world with the purpose of saving the world, also with the purpose—this in turn is implicit in his first purpose—of being the prototype . . . (PIC-238)

760.   What, then, is the difference between an admirer and an imitator? An imitator is or strives to be what he admires, and an admirer keeps himself personally detached, consciously or unconsciously does not discover that what is admired involves a claim upon him, to be or at least to strive to be what is admired. (PIC-241)

761.   . . . What dreadful untruth it is to admire in relation to the *truth* instead of imitating. . . . When there is no danger, when there is a dead calm, when everything is favorable to Christianity, it is all too easy to confuse an admirer with a follower, and this can happen very quietly; the admirer can die in the delusion that the position he took was the true one. Give heed, therefore, to contemporaneity. (PIC-245)

762.   And yet there is an infinite difference between an admirer and an imitator, because an imitator is, or at least strives to be, what he admires. (PIC-249)

763. They tried to demonstrate the truth of Christianity with reasons or by advancing reasons in relation to Christianity. And these reasons fostered doubt and doubt became the stronger. The demonstration of Christianity really lies in *imitation*. (FSE-68)

764. *Imitation, the imitation of Christ*, is really the point from which the human race shrinks. (JFY-188)

765. Christ is the prototype, to which corresponds *imitation*. There is really only one true way to be a Christian—to be a disciple. (JFY-207)

Silence/Stillness

766. Truth demands silence before it will raise its voice . . . (COI-210)

767. Only he who is silent will amount to anything. (R-145)

768. It does not harm the poor nobody to be abandoned if it helps him to find stillness. It is difficult . . . for the man of the world to find stillness; whether he is powerful or insignificant, it is difficult to find stillness in life's noise, difficult to find it where it is even when he himself does not bring the noise along with him. (TDIO-10)

769. Whoever says that he sought stillness but did not find it is an envious deceiver who wants to frustrate others, because otherwise he would be silent and sad or he would say, "I did not seek it properly; therefore I did not find it." . . . No, nothing except you yourself can take it [stillness] away from you; just as little as all the

world's power and all its wisdom and the united efforts of all humanity can give it to you, just as little can you yourself take it and give it away. (TDIO-11)

770.   . . . Without stillness conscience does not exist at all . . . (TDIO-11)

771.   Well, if one wishes to do nothing at all, one again escapes from the stillness into the stillness of spiritual death. (TDIO-39)

772.   Can anyone determine how long the silence must last before it can be said that now there is no more conversation . . . (WOL-307)

773.   How still, how secure everything is in God's house. . . . How much danger in this security! (CD-163)

774.   . . . Even more opposite to speaking than silence; he became a listener. (WA-12)

775.   Speech is the human being's advantage over the animal—yes, quite true, if he is able *to be silent*. (WA-13)

776.   If, however, you take time and listen more carefully, you hear—how amazing!—you hear silence. . . . In the distance you hear the familiar voice of the dog, you cannot say that this bellowing or this voice disturbs the silence. No, this belongs to the silence, is in a mysterious and thus in turn silent harmony with the silence; this increases it. (WA-13)

777.   . . . In the constant sociality of our day we shrink from solitude to the point . . . that no use for it is known other than as a punishment for criminals. (SUD-64)

778.   Do you not believe in silence? I do. When Cain had killed Abel, Abel was silent. But Abel's blood shouts to heaven, it shouts, it shouts to heaven . . . ah, the power of silence! (FSE-46)

779.   The first thing, the unconditional condition for anything to be done, consequently the very first thing that must be done is: create silence, bring about silence; God's Word cannot be heard, and if in order to be heard in the hullabaloo it must be shouted deafeningly with noisy instruments, then it is not God's Word; create silence! (FSE-47)

780.   Silence . . . does not consist simply in the absence of speaking. No, silence is like the subdued lighting in a pleasant room, like the friendliness in a modest living room; it is not something one talks about, but it is there and exercises its beneficent power. (FSE-48)

781.   A silence can have many different characteristics tending toward good or evil, but silence is ludicrous when it has the exasperating characteristic—that it speaks. This is very ludicrous: a silence that speaks, speaks very loudly, and says what it is concealing so that everyone can hear it, says precisely what one wishes to hide with the help of silence. (M-80)

782.   It is an awful satire, and an epigram on the materialism of our modern age, that nowadays the only use that can be made of solitude is imposing it as a penalty, as jail. (D-23)

783.   The guilt was . . . that he remained silent, not out of a sober-mindedness that remains silent when it is proper to remain silent, but out of a sagacity [cunning] that is silent because it is the most sagacious. (UDVS-150)

The Inner Self

784.   The phrase "know yourself' means: separate yourself from the other. (COI-177)

785.   . . . That we are not to read about or listen to or look at what is the highest and the most beautiful in life, but are, if you please, to live it. (E/O-138)

786.   When two people learn different things from life, it can be because they experience different things, but it can also be because they themselves were different. (EUD-22)

787.   . . . What one sees depends upon how one sees . . . (EUD-59)

788.   A person's inner being, then, determines what he discovers and what he hides. (EUD-60)

789.   The truly comic is that the infinite can be at work in a human being, and no one, no one discovers it by looking at him. (CUP-91)

790.   . . . Every speculative thinker confuses himself with humankind, whereby he becomes something infinitely great and nothing at all. (CUP-124)

791.   Christianity wants to give the single individual an eternal happiness, a good that is not distributed in bulk but only to one, and to one at a time. (CUP-130)

792.   In a world-historical dialectic, individuals fade away into humankind; in a dialectic such as that, it is impossible to discover you and me, an individual existing human being, even if new magnifying glasses for the concrete are invented. (CUP-350)

793.   The subjective thinker is not a scientist-scholar; he is an artist. To exist is an art. The subjective thinker is esthetic enough for his life to have esthetic content, ethical enough to regulate it, dialectical enough in thinking to master it. The subjective thinker's task is to *understand himself in existence*. (CUP-351)

794.   . . . The most dangerous traitor of all is the one every person has within himself. (WOL-23)

795.   . . . The sickbed and the nighttime hour preach more powerfully than all the orators, know this secret of speaking to you in such a way that you come to perceive that it is you who is being addressed, *you* in particular, not the one who is sitting beside you, not those outside, but *you* in particular, you who are feeling alone, alone in the whole world, alone in the midnight hour by the sickbed. . . . Death knows how to make itself understood . . . (CD-164)

796.   Ah, there is so much in the ordinary course of life that will lull a person to sleep, teach him to say "peace and no danger." Therefore we go to God's house to be awakened from sleep and to be pulled out of the spell. (CD-165)

797. . . . He the infinitely lofty one, is very close to you, closer than the people you have around you every day, closer than your most intimate friend before whom you feel that you can show yourself as you are. (CD-166)

798. Loftiness and distance seem to correspond to each other so that the person who is lofty is also distant from you. Equality and closeness also seem to correspond to each other so that the person who is close to you is also your equal. But when loftiness is very close to you and yet is loftiness, then you are in a difficult position. (CD-166)

799. But God in heaven, the infinitely lofty one or—yes, here it comes again—God, the knower of hearts, who is very close to you: God understands only one kind of honesty, that a person's life expresses what he says. (CD-167)

800. It is true, in Christ your sins are forgiven you, but this truth, which therefore is said also to each one individually, is yet in another sense still not true; it must be made into truth by each one individually. (WA-143)

801. The greatest hazard of all, losing the self, can occur very quietly in the world, as if it were nothing at all. No other loss can occur so quietly; any other loss—an arm, a leg, five dollars, a wife, etc.—is sure to be noticed. (SUD-32)

802. Immediacy actually has no self, it does not know itself; thus it cannot recognize itself and therefore generally ends in fantasy. . . . The man of immediacy does not know himself, he quite literally identifies himself only . . . by externalities . . . (SUD-53)

803. Earnestness is precisely this kind of honest distrust of oneself, to treat oneself as a suspicious character . . . (FSE-44)

804. It is not true of every narrow way that Christ is that way or that it leads to heaven. (FSE-66)

805. Compel a person to an opinion, a conviction, a belief— in all eternity, that I cannot do. But . . . I can compel him to become aware. (POV-50)

806. This I know, and I also know what it has cost, what I have suffered, which can be expressed by a single line: I was never like the others. Ah, of all the torments in youthful days, the most dreadful, the most intense: not to be like the others, never to live any day without painfully being reminded that one is not like the others, never to be able to run with the crowd, the desire and the joy of youth . . . (M-344)

Humility

807. This is why many a person prefers to be a philosopher, not a Christian, because to be a philosopher takes talent, to be a Christian humility, and anyone who so wills can have that. (E/O II-227)

808. This means: to be contented with being a human being, with being the humble one, the created being who can no more support himself than create himself. (UDVS-177)

809. Worldly worry always seeks to lead a human being into the small-minded unrest of comparisons. (UDVS-188)

810.   If human beings want to resemble God by ruling, they have forgotten God; then God has departed and they are playing the rulers in god's absence. This was paganism; this was human life in the absence of God. (UDVS-193)

811.   Courage makes the danger great and surmounts it, high-mindedness makes the wrong shabby and rises above it, patience makes the burden heavy and carries it, but meekness makes the burden light and carries it lightly. (UDVS-243)

812.   . . . It is, humanly speaking, unrewarding to be meek. . . . Courage gets paid with the visibility of the victory, high-mindedness with the pride of the glance, patience with the marks of suffering, but meekness is unrecognizable. (UDVS-243)

813.   The upbuilding is not for the healthy but for the sick, not for the strong but for the weak; thus for the presumably healthy and strong it is bound to appear at first as the terrifying. . . . So it is with the upbuilding, which at first is the terrifying; for the one without a broken and contrite heart, it is at first the crushing. (CD-96)

814.   When faith is seen from its one side, the heavenly, only the reflection of eternal salvation is seen in it; but seen from its other side, the merely human side, one sees sheer fear and trembling. (CD-175)

815.   Humanly, only the high and mighty person who has so many and such important things to think about speaks

this way. He says to his subordinate: you must yourself remind me so that I remember you. Alas, we say the same to you, you the Savior and Redeemer of the world. . . . We pray that you yourself will remind us of your suffering and death . . . (CD-275)

816.　. . . I am a penitent from whom God can demand everything. (M-402)

Existence

817.　I would rather be a swineherd out on Amager and be understood by swine than be a poet and be misunderstood by people. (E/O I-19)

818.　. . . Everything revolves around little things . . . (SOLW-89)

819.　Actuality is still not the tormentor that possibility is. (SOLW-329)

820.　How consistent life is! There is not anything that is true in one sphere that is not true in another. What profound earnestness that the laws of life are such that everyone must serve them whether he wants to or not. (SOLW-383)

821.　. . . "He is free who mocks his chains." (SOLW-421)

822.　. . . If the conclusion is lacking at the end, it is also lacking at the beginning. This should therefore have been said at the beginning. (CUP-13)

823.   . . . Can a historical point of departure be given for an eternal consciousness; . . . can an eternal happiness be built on historical knowledge? (CUP-15)

824.   The existing person continually has a *telos*. (CUP-313)

825.   . . . The only consistency outside Christianity is that of pantheism . . . (CUP-225)

826.   Existence is always the particular; the abstract does not exist. To conclude from this that the abstract does not have reality is a misunderstanding . . . (CUP-330)

827.   The true is not superior to the good and the beautiful, but the true and the good and the beautiful belong essentially to every human existence and are united for an existing person not in thinking them but in existing. (CUP-348)

828.   When the skeptic Zeno, for example, made a study of skepticism by trying, as existing, to remain unaffected by everything he encountered, so that, put to shame when he once went out of the way of a mad dog, he confessed that even a skeptical philosopher is still at times a human being . . . (CUP-352)

829.   Only the eternal can be and become and remain contemporary with every age. (WOL-31)

830.   Temporality itself, the whole of it, is a moment; eternally understood, temporality   is a moment, and a moment, eternally understood, is only once. (CD-98)

831. . . . The highest a person is capable of is to make an eternal truth true, to make it true that it is true—by doing it, by being oneself the demonstration, by a life that perhaps will also be able to convince others. (CD-98)

832. . . . With the help of eternity one suffers only once. (CD-100)

833. No, hardship can drown out every earthly voice; it is supposed to do just that, but it cannot drown out this voice of eternity deep within. (CD 109)

834. People continually think that it is the world, the environment, the circumstances, the situations that stand in one's way, in the way of one's fortune and peace and joy. Basically it is always the person himself who stands in his way . . . (CD-109)

835. For all true religiousness this is an extremely pernicious error that has its basis in our confusing becoming older in the sense of time with becoming older in the sense of eternity. (POV-48)

836. How does a crisis come about in the relationship of the spirit? Quite simply—by leaving out some intermediate links, by producing a conclusion and not giving the premises, but drawing a conclusion without first showing that of which it is the consequence . . . (M-432)

837. . . . The more meaningless we make life, the easier it is, and therefore . . . life in one sense has actually become easier, not, as the pastors falsify, by means of Christianity, but by means of abolishing Christianity. (M-457)

838.   It is quite true what Philosophy says: that Life must be understood backwards. But that makes one forget the other saying: that it must be lived—forwards. (D-111)

IX. Aspects of Life

Wealth

839.   It is unbelievable how sorrowful and debilitating a change takes place in a person as soon as he has taken comparison into his household. Comparison is a damnable guest whom no one is able to feed or satisfy, because it is ever more hungry and eats from the children's food. Comparison is the noisy resident in the previously quiet and calm house; comparison sleeps neither day nor night. (WOL-445)

840.   The bird lives on the *daily bread*, this heavenly food that is never stale, this enormous supply that is kept so well that no one can steal it, because the thief can steal only what "is saved over night"—what is used during the day no one can steal. (CD-13)

841.   What, then, does the poor Christian live on? On the *daily bread*. . . . But . . . the Christian, however poor he is, also has more to live on than the daily bread, which for him has something added, a worth and a sufficiency that it cannot have for the bird, because the Christian indeed prays for it and thus knows that the daily bread is *from God*. (CD-14)

842. . . . A human being is not differentiated from the bird by his inability to live on just as little but by his inability to live "on bread alone." He believes that it is the blessing that satisfies; yet what he seeks is not to become satisfied, but the blessing. (CD-15)

843. How poor not to be able to pray, how poor not to be able to give thanks, how poor to have to receive everything as if in ingratitude, how poor not to exist, as it were, for the benefactor to whom it owes its life! (CD-16)

844. Indeed, his wealth increases each time he prays and gives thanks, and each time it becomes clearer to him that he exists for God and God for him, whereas earthly wealth becomes poorer and poorer each time the rich man forgets to pray and to give thanks. (CD-16)

845. . . . There is very little to be found in Holy Scripture that answers this most important question [how to make a living in the "real world"]. (CD-19)

846. . . . What is the care of poverty but wanting to be rich! (CD-20)

847. But the thoughts of the one who wants to be rich are continually on the earth. . . . He is continually looking ahead—alas, ordinarily this is the best way to avoid temptation, but for him, yes, he does not know it, for him looking ahead is the very way to walk into the pitfall, the way to finding the temptation greater and greater and to sinking deeper and deeper into it. . . . Instead of *working* for the daily bread, which every human being is commanded to do, to *slave* for it . . . (CD-21)

848. Wealth and abundance come hypocritically in sheep's clothing under the guise of safeguarding against cares and then themselves become the object of care, become *the care*. (CD-23)

849. What God gives every day is—enough. (CD-23)

850. So the rich Christian *does have* abundance but is ignorant of it, and therefore he must *have become* ignorant. (CD-25)

851. The Christian, when he has abundance, is as one who does not have abundance. . . . With regard to abundance, thought can take the *thought of possession* away from the rich person, the thought that he possesses and owns his wealth and abundance as *his*. (CD-26)

852. Take the riches away, then I can no longer be called rich; but take tomorrow away—alas, then I can no longer be called rich either. . . (CD-27)

853. Losability is an essential feature of riches . . . (CD-27)

854. Everyone really knows well enough that in the more profound sense no human being owns anything, that no one has anything except what is given to him—basically everyone knows this. But the rich Christian bears in mind that he knows it . . . (CD-28)

855. . . . God has no objection to your releasing your debtors. . . . The unfaithfulness was that the steward dealt with someone else's property in this way. . . . The parable actually wants to teach that in this world the noble act is regarded as stupidity, the evil act as [cunning]. To cancel the debt, to steal from one's own pocket—how

stupid; but adroitly to steal from someone else's pocket—
how sagacious [cunning]! (CD-29)

856.   . . . The rich Christian has joy from his earthly wealth.
But is it not remarkable how much more quickly the
move was made from poverty to joy and, on the other
hand, how many difficulties were attached to moving
from earthly wealth to joy . . . (CD-30)

857.   . . . The life of holiness is lived in poverty, and thus in
turn in ignorance of all the wealth that is possessed.
(CD-30)

858.   The rich pagan, however, also has only one thought:
riches. . . . Not only is he without God in the world, but
wealth is his god, which attracts to itself his every
thought. (CD-31)

859.   . . . There has never lived a rich pagan who has obtained *enough*. (CD-35)

860.   A person is most healthy when he does not notice his
body at all or does not know he has a body, and the rich
person is healthy when healthy like the bird, he is not
aware of his earthly wealth . . . (CD-36)

861   It truly is the greatest wealth to be able to make others
rich . . . (CD-114)

862.   . . . The good of the spirit is communication [sharing].
(CD-116)

863.   . . . The way of perfection, to make others truly rich
must be: to communicate the goods of the spirit . . .
(CD-120)

The Esthetic

864. It is certainly not without reason that artists seldom or never paint a landscape by noonday light but more frequently by morning light. The distinctive freshness, the wonderful quivering, the exuberant changeableness of light and shadow evoke a particularly propitious total impression that does not permit any single point to be emphasized and, even though it were merely for the moment of discernment, to be divorced from the whole. Something similar happens in other spheres as well. We like to dwell on the first appearance of an idea in world history; we would like to have people from east and west come and worship it in its swaddling clothes . . . (EPW-36)

865. . . . Something is sought where one should not seek it; and what is worse, it is found where one should not find it. . . . Edified in the theater . . . esthetically stimulated in church. (E/O I-149)

866. . . . His whole life was intended for enjoyment. (E/O I-304)

867. . . . Who possess nothing except at the moment when they are showing it to others, who merely grasp the surface, not the essence. (E/O I-315)

868. What is glorious and divine about esthetics is that it is associated only with the beautiful. (E/O I-428)

869. That we are not to read about or listen to or look at what is the highest and the most beautiful in life, but are, if you please, to live it. (E/O II-139)

870.   . . . The relief that the esthetic sorrower alone craves: expression. (E/O II-234)

871.   The Christian view attributes everything to sin, something the philosopher is too esthetic to have the ethical courage to do. And yet this courage is the only thing that can rescue life and humankind . . . (E/O II-239)

872.   Thus when sin is brought into esthetics, the mood becomes either light-minded or melancholy . . . comic or tragic. (COA-14)

873.   The esthetic hero is great by *conquering*, the religious hero by *suffering*. (SOLW-454)

874.   There are three stages, an esthetic; an ethical; a religious . . . pleasure-perdition, action-victory, suffering. But despite this tripartition this book is nevertheless an either/or. (CUP-294)

875.   The ugliest person can make me utterly forget his external appearance by the fascination of the manifestation of his interior being. (TA-35)

876.   Someone really in love may be unable for a long time to describe his beloved; the predominating passion he deeply feels makes him forget how she looks when he is not looking at her. (TA-36)

877.   The world, after all, is so insipid that when it believes that one who proclaims the religious is someone who cannot produce the esthetic it pays no attention to the religious. (CD-415)

878. The esthetic always overrates youth and that moment of eternity; it cannot reconcile itself with the earnestness of the years, nor with the earnestness of eternity. Therefore the esthetic has always had a suspicion about the religious person, that he either has never had a sense for the esthetic or that basically he nevertheless would rather have continued belonging to it, but time exercised its deteriorating power, he became older, and then he turned to the religious. One divides life into two ages: the age of youth is the age of the esthetic; the older age is the age of religiousness—but to tell the truth we all would surely prefer to have continued to be young. (POV-47)

The Ethical

879. . . . I cannot imagine an unhappier or more tormented life than when a person has his duty outside himself and yet continually wants to carry it out. (E/O II-255)

880. The ethical individual, then, does not have duty outside himself but within himself. (E/O II-256)

881. . . . The ethical individual dares to employ the expression that he is his own editor, but he is also fully aware that he is responsible, responsible for himself personally, inasmuch as what he chooses will have a decisive influence on himself, responsible to the order of things in which he lives, responsible to God. (E/O II-260)

882. The fundamental point, therefore, is not whether a person can count on his fingers how many duties he has, but that he has once and for all felt the intensity of

duty in such a way that the consciousness of it is for him the assurance of the eternal validity of his being. (E/O II-266)

883. Every human being, then, can accomplish something; he can accomplish his task. (E/O II-296)

884. The ethical as such is the universal, and as the universal it applies to everyone, which from another angle means that it applies at all times. (FAT-54)

885. The tragic hero is still within the ethical. . . . Abraham's situation is different. By his act he transgressed the ethical altogether and had a higher *telos* outside it, in relation to which he suspended it. . . . Therefore, while the tragic hero is great because of his moral virtue, Abraham is great because of a purely personal virtue. (FAT-59)

886. The tragic hero does not enter into any private relationship to the divine . . . (FAT-60)

887. Where, then, is the field of honor? It is wherever a man falls with honor. (SOLW-353)

888. It is a contradiction to be willing to sacrifice one's life for a finite goal . . . (SOLW-410)

889. There is not always peril to life just because a person screams for help. (SOLW-466)

890. As soon as the will begins to cast a covetous eye on the outcome, the individual begins to become immoral . . . (CUP-135)

891.   How blessed to be able to fulfill God's requirements while smiling at the demands of the times. (CUP-138)

892.   The ethical is and remains the highest task assigned to every human being. (CUP-151)

893.   Ethically, what marks the deed the individual's own is the intention. . . . World-historically, I see the effect; ethically, I see the intention. (CUP-155)

894.   But the ethical is not only a knowing; it is also a doing that is related to a knowing . . . (CUP-160)

895.   . . . The ethical is quite consistently always very easy to understand. . . . But, in return, it is very difficult to accomplish—just the same for the sagacious as for the simple. (CUP-391)

896.   Hegelian philosophy has no ethics; therefore it has never occupied itself with the future, which is essentially the element or medium of ethics. (BOA-129)

897.   . . . Their [the bourgeois] *ethics* are a short summary of police ordinances; for them the most important thing is to be a useful member of the state, and to air their opinions in the club of an evening; they have never felt homesickness for something unknown and far away, nor the depth which consists in being nothing at all . . . *Journal* Jul 14, 1837 (KA-9)

The Religious

898.   A religiously developed person makes a practice of referring everything to God, of permeating and saturating every finite relation with the thought of God and thereby consecrating and ennobling it. (E/O II-43)

899.   The ethical expression for what Abraham did is that he meant to murder Isaac; the religious expression is that he meant to sacrifice Isaac . . . (FAT-30)

900.   It is only by faith that one achieves any resemblance to Abraham, not by murder. (FAT-31)

901.   . . . While for some individuals the religious is the absolute, for others it is not, and then goodnight to all meaning in life. (COA-106)

902.   . . . It is never good that something which is supposed to be sacred appears in ludicrous form. (SOLW-297)

903.   To be joyful out on 70,000 fathoms of water, many, many miles from all human help—yes, that is something great! To swim in the shallows in the company of waders is not the religious. (SOLW-470)

904.   . . . The issue is not about the truth of Christianity but about the individual's relation to Christianity. (CUP-15)

905.   . . . A highest good, called an eternal happiness, awaits me just as it awaits a housemaid and a professor. I have heard that Christianity is one's prerequisite for this good. I now ask how I may enter into relation to this doctrine. (CUP-15)

906.   . . . The only unforgivable high treason against Christianity is the single individual's taking his relation to it for granted. (CUP-16)

907.   The objective issue, then, would be about the truth of Christianity. The subjective issue is about the individual's relation to Christianity. Simply stated: How can I . . . share in the happiness that Christianity promises? (CUP-17)

908.   . . . The issue is rooted specifically in decision. (CUP-21)

909.   . . . The religious person is captive . . . (CUP-483)

910.   The contradiction is that becoming a Christian begins with the miracle of creation, and that this happens to someone who is created. (CUP-576)

911.   In relation to the absolute, there is only one time, the present; for the person who is not contemporary with the absolute, it does not exist at all. (PIC-60)

912.   What lifts up more, the thought of my own good deeds or the thought of God's grace? (JFY-153)

913.   That the Gospel's requirement should therefore be changed, that it should be scaled down, which sensibleness wants—to that I am heartily opposed, as is Christianity. . . . If the requirement is not the unconditioned, then I am not involved with God . . . (JFY-166)

914.   This is Christian piety: renouncing everything to serve God alone, to deny oneself in order to serve God alone—

and then to have to suffer for it—to do good and then to have to suffer for it. (JFY-169)

915. . . . While for some individuals the religious is the absolute, for others it is not, and then goodnight to all meaning in life. (COA-106)

916. No generation can endure without religion. (BOA-5)

917. . . . They have premises for living but do not arrive at any conclusion. . . . The lives of such people go on until death comes and puts an end to life, yet without, in the sense of a conclusion, bringing the end with it. (BOA-6)

918. A world-view, a life-view, is the only true conclusion to every production. . . . To use death as a conclusion is a paralogism . . . (BOA-8)

919. The religious sphere includes or ought to include the ethical . . . (BOA-21)

920. Christianity is the paradoxical truth; it is the paradox that the eternal once came into existence in time. (BOA-37)

921. All religiousness lies in subjectivity, in inwardness, in coming to oneself. (BOA-99)

922. In their religiousness the majority of people at most become present to themselves in a *past* or in a *future*, but not in a *present*. . . . They do not grasp that the religious is the *one thing needful*. . . . They understand very well that a person can die of hunger when he does not have

anything to live on, but they do not grasp that a human being lives on the Word that proceeds from the mouth of God. (BOA-105)

923.   Christianity can be communicated only by witnesses, i.e. by men who existentially express what they proclaim, realize it in their lives. (D-180)

Health

924.   Many people look upon having sorrow as one of life's conveniences. (E/O I-21)

925.   To make health the highest good is an animalistic principle; this is the way an animal is regarded—if it is not in good health, it is not worth anything. But man is spirit. To assert this principle is sin against the Holy Spirit, the most dreadful revolt against fellow-feeling. (SOLW-637)

926.   Alas, for the quack the untruth is all too true that it is the physician who needs the sick. (PIC-11)

Friendship

927.   The absolute condition for friendship is unity in a life-view. (E/O II-319)

928.   Unity in a life-view is the constituting element in friendship. If this is present, the friendship lasts even if the friend dies, inasmuch as the transfigured friend lives

on in the other; if this ceases the friendship is over even if the friend goes on living. (E/O II-321)

929.   Tell someone who your friends are, and he will know you . . . (EUD-253)

930.   . . . That the inwardness of truth is not the chummy inwardness with which two bosom friends walk arm in arm with each other but is the separation in which each person for himself is existing in what is true. (CUP-249)

931.   What communion between human being is the most deeply felt? The communion of suffering. Which of a person's communions is the most blessed? The communion with God. (CD-225)

932.   No, I can call God Father—even a little child does this—but the little child is not a friend of his father. I can call Christ my Savior, my Lord, my Redeemer, my benefactor, perhaps even my friend, but, please note, not in the sense that I dare call myself his friend . . . (M-424)

X. FAMILY

Romantic Love

933.   . . . Desire, as is known, is very sophistical. (E/O I-4)

934.   What does erotic love love? Infinity—What does erotic love fear? Boundaries. (E/O I-442)

935.   For it is this that distinguishes all love from lust: that it bears a stamp of eternity. (E/O II-21)

936.   The defect in earthly love is the same as its merit—that it is preference. (E/O II-62)

937.   To offer witticisms about the sexual is a paltry art, to admonish is not difficult, to preach about it in such a way that the difficulty is omitted is not hard, but to speak humanly about it is an art. (COA-67)

938.   . . . Erotic love expresses itself in loving a one and only, a one and only in the whole world . . . (SOLW-36)

939.   Who says that a seducer was a seducer at the very first moment? No, he became that at the second moment. (SOLW-103)

940.   . . . It is comic that Don Juan has 1,003 mistresses, for the number simply indicates that they have no value. (SOLW-293)

941.   . . . Inwardness in erotic love does not mean to get married seven times to Danish girls, and then to go for the French, the Italian, etc., but to love one and the same and yet be continually renewed in the same erotic love, so that it continually flowers anew in mood and exuberance—which, when applied to communication, is the inexhaustible renewal and fertility of expression. (CUP-259)

942.   . . . Where a seducer does not sing *to* the girl but *for* the girl, using this means to stimulate her imagination. (CA-33)

943.   . . . In all seduction it holds true: too speedy a plunge and all is lost. (CA-34)

944.   . . . If one considers a single girl at a time, one cannot look enough at such a lovely little lass, with her wise, saucy, affectionate eyes; but a whole school of girls—well, I will not say another word. (CA-76)

945.   . . . For what is a woman's loveliness if it is for sale for money? (CA-157)

946.   Modesty and chastity certainly cannot make a girl beautiful, but beauty cannot make a harlot beautiful, simply because she is essentially unbeautiful, whereas the chaste and modest girl lacks beauty only accidentally. (CA-163)

947.   Passion always has this unconditional characteristic—that it excludes the third. (WOL-50)

948.   . . . By the sensuous, the flesh, Christianity understands selfishness. (WOL-50)

949.   . . . Erotic love is undeniably life's most beautiful happiness and friendship the greatest temporal good! (WOL-267)

Love

950.   The romantic longing for something higher may well be genuine, but just as man must not separate what God has joined together, so man also must not join what God has separated . . . (COI-329)

951.   The highest enjoyment imaginable is to be loved, loved more than anything else in the world. (E/O I-368)

952.   I meditate upon how proportionately God shares with man, for it must be far more difficult for him to love a human being in such a way that he is not crushed by God's love, far more difficult for him to make himself so small that a human being really can love him. (E/O I-495)

953.   Every feeling, every mood, gains a higher meaning for me by having her share in it. (E/O II-9)

954.   Love is self-giving . . . (E/O II-109)

955.   If duty is hard, *eh bien*, then love pronounces it, actualized it, and thereby does more than the duty; if love is about to become so soft that it cannot be kept stable, duty sets boundaries to it. (E/O II-149)

956.   . . . Only in love is the different made equal . . . (PF-25)

957.   . . . For erotic love is jubilant when it unites equal and equal and is triumphant when it makes equal in erotic love that which was unequal. (PF-27)

958.   . . . For it is indeed less terrifying to fall upon one's face while the mountains tremble at the god's voice than to sit with him as his equal, and yet the god's concern is precisely to sit this way (PF-34)

959.   . . . The lovers were set free by belonging to each other . . . (TDIO-43)

960. . . . Love is older than everything else . . . because when it exists it seems as if it has existed for a long time; it presupposes itself back into the distant past until all searching ends in the inexplicable origin. (TDIO-47)

961. . . . Lovers always hate a third party . . . reflection is always a third party. (SOLW-33)

962. The person who listens to the talk of several lovers will learn that no two say the same thing, although they all speak about the same thing. (SOLW-35)

963. . . . The lover cannot explain anything at all. . . . The lovable is the inexplicable. (SOLW-36)

964. . . . To love is to see the beautiful. (SOLW-141)

965. If love is assumed to have happily undergone infinite reflection, then it is something different, then it is religious . . . (SOLW-414)

966. It never occurs to a girl truly in love that she has purchased her happiness at too high a price, but rather that she has not purchased it at a price high enough. (CUP-231)

967. . . . Objectivity is not a lover's crown of honor. (CUP-577)

968. Being in love is the culmination of a person's purely human existence, which is a double existence, and for that very reason being in love is simultaneously just as much inwardness as it is a relation directed outwardly to actuality. (TA-49)

969.   The person who truly loves does not love once for all
       . . . No he loves with all his love; it is totally present in
       every expression; he continually spends all of it, and
       yet he continually keeps it all in his heart. . . . When
       the lover spends all his love, he keeps it whole . . .
       (UDVS-30)

970.   Indeed, what has the person actually lost who, because
       of his love, became a victim of human deception if it
       turns out in eternity that love remains, whereas the de-
       ception has ended! (WOL-6)

971.   . . . One can do works of love in an unloving, yes, even
       in a self-loving way . . . (WOL-13)

972.   . . . This is the very mark of Christian love and is its
       distinctive characteristic—that it contains this appar-
       ent contradiction to love is a duty. (WOL-24)

973.   If anyone thinks he is a Christian and yet is indifferent
       toward being that, then he really is not one at all. In-
       deed, what would we think of a person who gave assur-
       ances that he was in love and also that it was a matter of
       indifference to him? (WOL-25)

974.   . . . For the very enigma of love is this—that there is no
       higher certainty than the beloved's renewed assurances.
       In the human sense, to be absolutely certain of being
       loved is not to love, since this means to stand above the
       relationship . . . (WOL-157)

975.   Is it loving the person you see if you at every moment
       look at him, testing . . . (WOL-166)

976. Thus, for his own sake the lover wishes to remain in debt; he does not wish exemption from any sacrifice, far from it. (WOL-178)

977. *As soon as love dwells on itself, it is out of its element.* (WOL-182)

978. So it is also with love. If you wish to maintain love, you must maintain it in the infinitude of the debt. Therefore beware of comparison! (WOL-186)

979. But can one human being implant love in another human being's heart? . . . It is God, the Creator, who must implant love in each human being, he who himself is Love. (WOL-216)

980. Just by unconditionally not requiring the slightest reciprocal love, the one who truly loves has taken an unassailable position; he can no more be deceived out of his love than a man can be tricked out of the money he tenders as a gift and gives to someone. (WOL-242)

981. Love does not seek its own; it rather gives in such a way that the gift looks as if it were the recipient's property . . . The one who loves also knows how to make himself unnoticed so that the person helped does not become dependent upon him . . . (WOL-274)

982. To love people is the only thing worth living for, and without this love you are not really living. (WOL-375)

983. Does not even an otherwise humble gift, an insignificant little something, have infinite worth for the lover when it is from the beloved! (CD-15)

984. Love is the firmest of all bonds, since it makes the lover one with what he loves. (CD-84)

985. Is this not an excellent way to test how glorious a good is for one, this: how much one has given up for its sake? (CD-177)

986. If there was one lover who in the most beautiful and glowing terms praised the beloved's perfections and merits, and if there was a second lover who did not say a single word about this but merely said, "For her sake I have left everything"—which of these two would speak more gloriously in her praise! (CD-177)

987. Alas, but to betray is the most painful blow you can inflict upon love; there is no suffering, not even the most excruciating physical suffering, in which love agonizes as it agonizes soulfully in being betrayed, because for love there is nothing as blessed as faithfulness! (CD-279)

988. . . . The true expression of loving much is just to forget oneself completely. (WA-140)

989. Lord Jesus Christ, you who certainly did not come to the world in order to judge, yet by being love that was not loved you were a judgment upon the world. (WA-169)

990. Usually it is presented this way: justice, this is the severe judgment; love is leniency, which does not judge. . . . No, no, love's judgment is the most severe judgment. (WA-170)

991.   . . . Love is always joyous, particularly when it sacrifices everything . . . (SUD-127)

992.   And just as it so beautifully happens with lovers that they begin to resemble each other . . . (PIC-189)

993.   A true love affair is indeed also a restless thing, but it never enters the lover's head to want to change things as they are. (FSE-21)

994.   Indeed, how could it occur to the God of love to will to compel to be loved! (M-294)

Marriage

995.   All the beauty implicit in the erotic of paganism has its validity in Christianity insofar as it can be combined with marriage. (E/O II-10)

996.   Marriage, then ought not to call forth erotic love; on the contrary, it presupposes it not as something past but as something present. (E/O II-36)

997.   Pride can be portrayed very well, because what is essential in pride is not sequence but intensity in the moment. Humility is hard to portray precisely because it is sequence. . . . Romantic love can be portrayed very well in the moment; marital love cannot, for an ideal husband is not one who is ideal once in his life, but one who is that every day. (E/O II-135)

998.   He [a married man] solves the great riddle, to live in eternity and yet to hear the cabinet clock strike in such a way that its striking does not shorten but lengthens his eternity . . . (E/O II-138)

999.   It is not the seducers who do harm to marriage, but cowardly married men. (E/O II-281)

1000. Many a marriage has been profaned, and not by a stranger. (COA-71)

1001. . . . Marriage will take away the romantic fancies and illusions and provide a secure abode for erotic love within the impregnable fortress of duty and give the resolved one new enthusiasm and in the course of time daily wonder over his happiness. (TDIO-56)

1002. The resolution of marriage is that love conquers every-thing. Yes, it conquers everything, but it does perish in adversity if no resolution holds it firm, it perishes in prosperity if no resolution holds it firm, it degenerates in the everyday if no resolution encourages it, it is stifled in imagined importance if no resolution humbles it. (TDIO-62)

1003. So, then, a true conception of life and of oneself is re-quired for the resolution of marriage; but this already implies the second great requirement, which is just like the first: *a true conception of God*. . . . This language is the resolution, the only language in which God will involve himself with a human being. And thus a language is required in which they talk with each other . . . (TDIO-63)

1004.   . . . Marriage is and remains the most important voyage of discovery a human being undertakes; compared with a married man's knowledge of life, any other knowledge of it is superficial . . . (SOLW-89)

1005.   . . . Alongside her through whom I feel the meaning of my life. (SOLW-93)

1006.   . . . For only a married man is an authentic man . . . (SOLW-93)

1007.   Marriage I regard, then, as the highest goal of individual life . . . (SOLW-101)

1008.   . . . For if the lovers' union is not a marriage from the beginning, it never becomes that. (SOLW-105)

1009.   . . . If because of its responsibility marriage is an epic, then because of its happiness it certainly is also an idyll. (SOLW-117)

1010.   . . . So is marriage's door always shut, because a divine service is going on continually. (SOLW-118)

1011.   The ideal beauty is veiled beauty . . . (SOLW-123)

1012.   . . . And only in marriage does being in love have its true expression; outside marriage it is seduction or flirtation. (SOLW-126)

1013.   She loves her husband so much that she always wants him to be dominant, and this is why he appears to be so strong and she so weak, for she uses her strength to

support him, uses it as devotedness and submission.
What wonderful weakness! (SOLW-144)

1014.   . . . A union of people who separately are weak, a union
as unbeautiful and depraved as a child-marriage. (TA-
106)

1015.   That a particular kind of love is Christianly made a matter of conscience is sufficiently known to everyone. We
are speaking about marriage. (WOL-137)

1016.   I was an eternity too old for her. (D-42)

Children

1017.   Bring up your children well, and you will come to know
what you owe your parents. (E/O II-76)

1018.   The child is astonished at insignificant things. The adult
has laid aside childish things, he has seen the wondrous,
but it amazes him no more. . . . There is truly only one
eternal object of wonder—that is God. (EUD-226)

1019.   One can be thirty years old and more, forty years old,
and still be just a child—yes, one can die as an aged
child. (EUD-316)

1020.   One learns wonder from a child and fear from an adult
. . . (TDIO-25)

1021.   If someone were to memorize the Bible, there could be
something beautiful inasmuch as there was something
childlike in his behavior, but essentially the adult learns

only by appropriating, and he essentially appropriates the essential only by doing it. (TDIO-39)

1022. As long as one is a child one has enough imagination . . . when we are adults, imagination tends to make us bored. (SOLW-27)

1023. An adult may very well join in children's play with total interest, may be the one who really makes the game lively, but he still does not play as a child. (CUP-413)

1024. What is it that makes the child's life so easy? It is that so often "quits" can be called and a new beginning is so frequently made. (CUP-550)

1025. Christianity cannot be poured into a child, because it always holds true that every human being grasps only what he has use for, and the child has no decisive use for Christianity. (CUP-590)

1026. There is no lack of examples of people who themselves have not previously been religiously moved but are now so moved by a child. But this piety is not the religiousness that should essentially belong to an adult . . . (CUP-591)

1027. This parental piety and the child's teachability and ease of understanding this blessedness are lovely and lovable, but it is not really Christianity. It is Christianity in the medium of fantasy-perception; it is a Christianity from which the terror has been removed; the *innocent* child is led to God or Christ. (CUP-591)

1028. . . . The child has no consciousness of sin and therefore is a sinner without the consciousness of sin. (CUP-592)

1029. The child's receptivity is so entirely without decision . . . (CUP-601)

1030. We best learn to know children when we watch them play, and young people when we hear them wish. . . . To choose is the earnestness of life. . . . There is no mirror as accurate as the wish. (UDVS-248)

1031. Possibility is like a child's invitation to a party; the child is willing at once, but the question now is whether the parents will give permission—and as it is with the parents, so it is with necessity. (SUD-37)

Women

1032. Hardly was man created before we find Eve already as audience at the snake's philosophical lectures, and we see that she mastered them with such ease that at once she could utilize the results of the same in her domestic practice. (EPW-3)

1033. . . . Xanthippe is still remembered as a pattern of feminine eloquence and as founder of a school that has lasted to this very day, whereas Socrates' school has long since disappeared. (EPW-3)

1034. Yet many centuries elapsed before woman's great abilities were *properly* recognized. This was reserved for France, and here we shall refer solely to two phenomena: that reason in the French Revolution was represented by a female and that the Saint-Simonists placed them on a totally equal footing with the men. If to this we now add the fact that no one has ever yet succeeded in getting the better of a lady in an argument . . . then one certainly comprehends her superiority in intellectual matters . . . (EPW-3)

1035. With pleasure I look forward to the time when the ladies will know how to make clear to themselves what love really is, [and] will probe deeply into the secrets of the Trinity (although this doctrine will be especially difficult for them, because hitherto they have had a bad time grasping that two can agree). (EPW-4)

1036. But what can more truthfully be called a woman's life than her love? (E/O I-172)

1037. A woman comprehends the finite; she understands it from the ground up. That is why she is exquisite . . . lovely . . . happy . . . in harmony with existence. . . . Woman explains the finite; man pursues the infinite. . . . That is why I hate all that detestable rhetoric about the emancipation of women. (E/O II-311)

1038. . . . According to Xenophon . . . he [Socrates] had the same benefit from this shrewish woman [Xanthippe] as trainers have from wild horses, the benefit of learning to constrain them, that for him she was an exercise in controlling mankind . . . (TDIO-192)

1039. It is the man's function to be absolute, to act absolutely, to express the absolute; the woman consists in the relational. (SOLW-48)

1040. . . . Honesty is the best policy, only not when it comes to pleasing women. (SOLW-338)

XI. Society

Time and Eternity

1041. But when time itself is the task, it is a defect to finish ahead of time. (CUP-164)

1042. Only the eternal applies at all times . . . is always true, pertains to every human being of whatever age . . . (UDVS-9)

1043. But with respect to the eternal, no time ever comes when a person has outgrown it or has grown older—than the eternal! If there is something eternal in a human being, then the discourse about it must be different; it must say that there is something that should always have its time, something that a person should always do . . . (UDVS-11)

1044. No, human language calls it maturity and an advantage to have outgrown, as an adult, the childish and the youthful, but to want at any time to have outgrown the eternal it calls falling away from God and perdition . . . (UDVS-12)

1045. It is eternally false that guilt becomes something different even if a century passed by; to say anything like that is to confuse the eternal with what the eternal least resembled, with human forgetfulness. (UDVS-18)

1046. . . . The eternal, if one grasps it is truth, is the only, unconditionally the only thing of which one may unconditionally say: It is never regretted. (UDVS-114)

1047.   . . . The human being . . . is the place where the eternal and the temporal continually touch each other, where the eternal is refracted in the temporal. (UDVS-194)

1048.   The basic meaning of human deliberating is to weigh the temporal against the eternal; in all other human deliberating this basic meaning must be present. (UDVS-309)

1049.   There is scarcely any more upside-down thought than this, that the eternal is the uncertain, and scarcely any more upside-down sagacity than that which lets go of the eternal—because it is the uncertain, and grasps the temporal—because it is the certain. (CD-134)

1050.   . . . To bring eternity a little closer, is decisive for every sufferer if he is to be comforted. (CD-135)

1051.   *Only the temporal can be lost temporally;* temporality as such cannot possibly take away from you anything other than the temporal . . . . If the terrible thing happens that a person *temporally* loses *the eternal,* we are no longer talking about *loss*—this is *perdition.* (CD-136)

1052.   . . . *Only the eternal can be gained eternally.* (CD-137)

1053.   . . . Do not doubt whether you are immortal—tremble, because you are immortal. (CD-203)

1054.   . . . Immortality and judgment are one and the same. (CD-204)

1055.   Immortality is judgment, or the separation between the righteous and the unrighteous. . . . What, then, is the eternal? It is the difference between right and wrong. All else is transitory . . . (CD-207)

1056. His innocent sacrifice is not past even though the cup of suffering is empty, is not a bygone event although it is past, is not an event finished and done with although it was eighteen hundred years ago, would not become that even if it were eighteen thousand years ago. (CD-278)

1057. Consequently we dare not wash our hands—at least we cannot do it except as Pilate could do it; consequently we are not spectators and observers at a past event—we are indeed accomplices in a present event. (CD-278)

1058. We have Christ's word that there is an eternal life, and with that the matter is decided. (WA-102)

1059. We have made the finite and the infinite, the eternal and the temporal, the highest and the lowest, blend in such a way that it is impossible to say which is which, or the situation is an impenetrable ambiguity. (JFY-123)

1060. . . . An eternal truth that from first to last is equally true, no more true in its latest moment than in its first. . . . A hypothesis is shy at the beginning; then it flaunts the years, but in return it is also liable to annihilation at any moment. (BOA-36)

1061. They want to demonstrate the truth and the trustworthiness of the eternal by means of what is infinitely deceitful: the years and the human crowd. . . . Christianity is the paradoxical truth; it is the paradox that the eternal once came into existence in time. (BOA-37)

1062. The "historical" in Christianity vs. the "History" of Christianity. (BOA-38)

1063. The essentially Christian has no history, because the essentially Christian is this paradox, that God once came into existence in time. This is the offense, but also the point of departure; whether it is eighteen hundred years ago or yesterday, one can equally well be contemporary with it. (BOA-40)

1064. . . . The person who believes it if it happened eighteen hundred years ago can just as well believe it if it happens today—unless he believes it *because* it was eighteen hundred years ago, which is *not* to believe *at all*. (BOA-46)

1065. . . . That which in temporality must be an enigma and which only eternity can and will explain. (BOA-227)

Academia

1066. . . . You are not supposed to learn from your inferiors. (E/O-131)

1067. . . . In many places Hegel behaved irresponsibly—not toward grocers, who believe only half of what a person says anyway, but toward enthusiastic youths who believed him. (CUP-118)

1068. . . . That through Hegel a system, the absolute system, was brought to completion—without having an ethics. (CUP-118)

1069. In committee deliberations, it is quite all right to include a dissenting vote, but a system that has a dissenting vote as a paragraph within it is a queer monstrosity. (CUP-123)

1070. Hegelian philosophy has canceled the principle of contradiction . . . (CUP-304)

1071. Therefore be cautious with an abstract thinker who not only wants to remain in abstraction's pure being but wants this to be the highest for a human being, and wants such thinking, which results in the ignoring of the ethical and a misunderstanding of the religious, to be the highest human thinking. (CUP-307)

1072. . . . To think abstractly is easier than to exist . . . (CUP-308)

1073. The endorsement of ethics is what every existing person has a legitimate right to demand of all that is called wisdom. (CUP-309)

1074. The most dangerous skepticism is always that which least appears as such . . . (CUP-310)

1075. . . . In our day . . . one becomes a professor, is knighted, and is married, through communicating "doubt about everything" as an article of faith to believing listeners. (JFY-119)

1076. No, Christ did not appoint professors, but followers. If Christianity is not reduplicated in the life of the person expounding it, then he does not expound Christianity . . . (D-116)

1077.   The stone which was rolled before Christ's tomb might appropriately be called *the philosopher's stone* because its removal gave not only the Pharisees but, now for 1800 years, the philosophers so much to think about. *Journal* Nov 25, 1834 (KA-2)

Clergy

1078.   . . . How rarely faith is perhaps found among the clergy! (CUP-132)

1079.   A penetrating religious renunciation of the world and what is of the world, adhered to in daily self-denial, would be inconceivable to the youth of our day; every second theological graduate, however, has enough virtuosity to do something far more marvelous. He is able to found a social institution with no less a goal than to save all who are lost. (TA-71)

1080.   The trouble is not that Christianity is not voiced (thus the trouble is not that there are not enough pastors) but that it is voiced in such a way that the majority eventually think it utterly inconsequential. (SUD-102)

1081.   It applies even to the pastors in "established Christendom" that they do not so much "confess Christ" as "it is known of them." . . . (PIC-219)

1082.   The Christian sermon today has become mainly "observations." (PIC-233)

1083.   Christianity has of course known very well what it wanted. It wants to be proclaimed by *witnesses*—that is, by persons who proclaim the teaching and also existentially express it. (PIC-288)

1084. Since therefore we know the fear of the Lord we seek to win men (2 Cor 5: 11). To begin instantly or to want *first of all* to win people may even be profane, in any case worldliness, not Christianity, no more than it is fear of God. No, let your effort *first*, let it first and foremost, express that you fear God. (FSE-xx)

1085. The person who is going to preach ought to live in the Christian thoughts and ideas; they ought to be his daily life. (FSE-10)

1086. One can also speak so loftily that one says nothing at all. (FSE-26)

1087. I will earn my bread by, for example, proclaiming Christianity. . . . This is my livelihood; it is not for the sake of Christianity that I obtained a livelihood—it is for my own sake. Truly, it is not at all dangerous for the congregation to find out what it does indeed know—that I, too, am a human being who needs something to live on. (JFY-126)

1088. The dangerous thing is that I attire myself in a solemnness and dignity, that it is for the sake of Christianity—as if it were Christianity that stood in need of my obtaining a livelihood and making a career, as if it were not rather that I need an indulgence from Christianity for making my proclamation of Christianity into a livelihood in this way. (JFY-127)

1089.   . . . *Witnesses to the truth*, who did not, and together with a family, live off the doctrine but lived and died for the doctrine. (JFY-129)

1090.   . . . What one's life proclaims is a hundred thousand times more powerfully effective than what one's mouth proclaims . . . (JFY-132)

1091.   Even if not one single person wants to accept it, Christianity remains unchanged; it does not yield a jot or tittle; if everyone were to accept it, not a jot or tittle may be changed. It is God's love for mankind that Christianity proclaims, for every single person, the most impoverished, the most wretched, the most forsaken. For that one person, God in his love has, as it were, set heaven and earth in motion, but if all human beings who ever lived or are living joined together to demand just one jot or tittle of change—no, never! (JFY-156)

1092.   Thus the unconditioned requirement becomes a Sunday ceremony, an entertainment put on by the pastors—and a person's life otherwise continues in total security, unmoved by the wounding restlessness of the unconditioned requirement. (JFY-159)

1093.   People even have a perhaps groundless anxiety about calling the pastor, who quite possibly in our day would talk somewhat like a physician anyway—so one calls the physician. (JFY-202)

1094.   The first condition for winning people is that the communication reaches them. (JFY-224)

1095. From a religious point of view, speaking ought essentially to be *ex tempore* also for this reason. This way a person is unable to have at his disposal all those cunning and cautious turns and shadings of speech with which one protects oneself, but it is just right for one to come out with it. (JFY-225)

1096. Beware of those who go about in long robes. It is unnecessary to say that Christ does not mean these words to be a criticism of their clothing. . . . If the professional apparel for pastors had been short robes, then Christ would have said: Beware of those in short robes. . . . It is at the profession, which he characterizes by its special costume (for he has a completely different understanding of what it is to be a teacher), that he wants to strike. Beware of those who *like* to go about in long robes. (M-198)

1097. The monastic candidate nevertheless made himself homogeneous with the world, for he allowed himself and his way to be regarded as the extraordinary. (M-420)

1098. Christianity received its first blow when the emperor became a Christian. The second, and far more dangerous blow, came when the category of the directly recognizable extraordinary Christian emerged. The error lay, as stated, not in entering the monastery but in the title of extraordinary Christian, which was directly honored with admiration by the contemporaries. (M-421)

1099. Therefore preaching should not be done in churches but in the street, right in the middle of life, the actuality of ordinary, daily life. (M-535)

1100. It is just like wanting to be regarded as a courageous man, and then in the evening, when it is dark, wanting to have someone accompany him because one does not dare to walk alone in the dark. A truth-witness who has others to defend him! (M-595)

1101. A modern clergyman . . . is an active, adroit, quick person who, in beautiful language, with an attractive presence, etc., knows how very lightly to introduce a little Christianity, but very lightly, as lightly as possible. (M-454)

1102. . . . A night watchman shouts too loudly and disturbs the inhabitants' quiet and sleep. But there is no complaint about the clergy; they reassure the congregation in regard to their salvation! (BOA-48)

1103. Educated as Adler is by some Hegelian dialectic, it is not strange that he himself is living in the delusion that these three designations (an apostle, a religiously awakened person, an enthusiast) are more or less one and the same, or that in explanation the one can be exchanged for the other. (BOA-60)

1104. . . . What a satire on humanity that the more the preaching of the Good Tidings deteriorates, the wider the circulation it receives by means of ever new inventions. (D-25)

1105. One thing is to suffer; another to graduate and become a professor in someone else's sufferings. (D-176)

1106. Christianity can be communicated only by witnesses, i.e. by men who existentially express what they proclaim, realize it in their lives. (D-180)

Bible Scholarship

1107. "There is no problem as far as I am concerned; I certainly intend to comply—as soon as the discrepancies are ironed our and the interpreters agree fairly well." Aha! That certainly will not be for a long time yet. . . . What a tragic issue of scholarship . . . (FSE-32)

1108. If you are a scholar, remember that if you do not read God's Word in another way, it will turn out that after a lifetime of reading God's Word many hours every day, you nevertheless have never read—God's Word. (FSE-33)

1109. But how is God's Word read in Christendom? . . . The majority never read God's word, a minority read it more or less learnedly, that is, nevertheless do not read God's Word but observe the mirror [the mirror itself, not their appearance in it]. (FSE-33)

1110. It takes a personality, an *I* to look at oneself in a mirror. . . . No, while reading God's Word you must incessantly say to yourself: It is I to whom it is speaking; it is I about whom it is speaking. (FSE-44)

1111. It is all just as easy to understand as the remark "The weather is fine today," a remark that could become difficult to understand in only one way—if a literature came into existence in order to interpret it. (FSE-34)

1112. It seems as if all this research and pondering and scrutinizing would draw God's Word very close to me; the truth is that this is the very way, this is the most cunning way, to remove God's Word as far as possible from me . . . (FSE-35)

1113. Paganism required: know yourself. Christianity declares: No, that is provisional—know yourself—and then look at yourself in the mirror of the Word in order to know yourself properly. No true self-knowledge without God-knowledge or [without standing] before God. To stand before the mirror means to stand before God. (JFY-234)

The Bible

1114. The first requirement is that you must not look at the mirror, observe the mirror, but must see yourself in the mirror. (FSE-25)

1115. . . . When you are reading God's Word, it is not the obscure passages that bind you but what you understand and with that you are to comply at once. (FSE-29)

1116. . . . The person who is not alone with God's Word is not reading God's Word. (FSE-30)

1117. . . . I thereby also make sure that God's Word cannot take hold of me because I do not place myself in any personal relation to the Word. . . . That the Word would take hold of me, precisely me, gain power over me so that I could not defend myself against it, so that it would go on pursuing me until I either acted according to it, renouncing the world, or at least admitted that I did not do it. . . . When you read God's Word, in everything you read, continually to say to yourself: It is I to whom it is speaking, it is I about whom it is speaking—this is earnestness, precisely this is earnestness. (FSE-36)

1118. Then the prophet says to him, "Thou art the man." See, the tale the prophet told was a story, but this "Thou art the man"—this was another story—this was the transition to the subjective. (FSE-38)

1119. . . . He can listen to the prophet's tale and pretend as if nothing has happened—until the prophet, weary of this impersonality and objectivity, so extolled in our age as culture and earnestness, uses his authority and says: Thou art the man. (FSE-39)

1120. One makes God's Word into something impersonal, objective, a doctrine—instead of its being the voice of God that you shall hear. (FSE-39)

1121. . . . . To the degree to which we are all Christians, to that degree the New Testament is no longer the truth. (M-115)

1122. Yet the New Testament is a strange book; it is always right, even if the opposite seems to be the case. (M-455)

1123. An apostle is not born; an apostle is a man who is called and appointed by God and sent by him on a mission. (BOA-176)

1124. I am not to listen to Paul because he is brilliant or matchlessly brilliant, but I am to submit to Paul because he has divine authority . . . (BOA-177)

1125. Authority is a specific quality that enters from somewhere else and qualitatively asserts itself precisely when the content of the statement or the act is made a matter of indifference esthetically. (BOA-179)

1126. Is knowledge higher than faith? By no means. (BOA-213)

1127. . . . Is it not self-contradictory to accept a part of the Bible as God's word, accept Christianity as divine teaching—and then, when confronted with something you cannot bring into accord with your intelligence or your emotions to say that God is contradicting Himself . . . (D-166)

Church

1128. . . . To belong to the visible Church has become very doubtful testimony that one actually is a Christian. (CUP-364)

1129. That one can know what Christianity is without being a Christian must, then, be answered in the affirmative. Whether one can know what it is to be a Christian without being one is something else, and it must be answered in the negative. (CUP-372)

1130. . . . There is an enormous difference between knowing what Christianity is and being a Christian. (CUP-380)

1131. What Christ required as a condition for coming into the situation in which there can be any question of becoming a Christian, a decisive action—that is not needed anymore. A person's life is essentially homogeneous with the secular mentality and this world. So one perhaps hears a little about something that perhaps is Christianity; one reads a little, thinks a little about Christianity, experiences a mood once in a while . . . (JFY-194)

1132. But I and everyone else must be measured by the ideal; according to the ideal it will be determined where I am. It must not be that we human beings are permitted to abolish the ideal requirements, saying that it is not something for us, and then to find a certain mediocrity and to begin there and make that the criterion, and then perhaps even to become distinguished—precisely because the yardstick has been converted to our size. (JFY 199)

1133. Finally people become bored with Christianity, since the pressure of *imitation* was lacking, the ideal, Christ as the prototype. (JFY-201)

1134. The ordinary kind of Christianity is: a secularized life, avoiding major crimes more out of sagacity [cunning] than for the sake of conscience, ingeniously seeking the pleasures of life—and then one in a while a so-called pious mood. (JFY-202)

1135. The good news of the Gospel is not to be foisted on people by means of demonstrations and reasons, demeaningly, as when a mother must sit and beg her child to eat the good wholesome food, but he turns up his nose at it and does not really care to eat. No, the appetite has to be aroused. (JFY 203)

Secular Society

1136. Precisely because politicians overlook continuity, they admit only two of the three marks of the validity of the public spirit, *consensus* and *universalitas* (and even these in a rather trivial and arbitrary sense), but completely overlook the third—*antiquitas*. (EPW-215)

1137. Thus it is a love without any real content, and the eternity so frequently talked about is nothing but what could be called the eternal moment of enjoyment, an infinity that is no infinity . . . (COI-300)

1138. The world is rejuvenated, but as Heine so wittily remarked, it was rejuvenated by romanticism to such a degree that it became a baby again. (COI-304)

1139. If I let the human race create God, then there is no conflict between God and man; if I let man disappear in God, then there is no conflict, either. (COI-314)

1140. When the great perishes in the world, this is tragic . . . (COI-322)

1141. . . . Although everyone wants to rule, no one wants to have responsibility. (E/O I-142)

1142. Our age reminds one very much of the disintegration of the Greek State; everything continues, and yet there is no one who believes in it. The invisible spiritual bond that gives it validity has vanished. (E/O II-19)

1143. . . . In modern drama the bad is always represented by the most brilliantly gifted characters, whereas the good, the upright, is represented by the grocer's apprentice. (E/O II-228)

1144. Alas, a person can encumber his soul not only with meat and drink but also with the world's honor and people's admiration. (EUD-151)

1145. The world can be possessed only by its possessing me, and this in turn is the way it possesses the person who has won the world . . . (EUD-164)

1146. One who esteems the temporal will gradually be rendered incapable of being attentive to the eternal, and one in whose eyes the things of this earth remain estimable will gradually lose the capacity to prize the things of heaven. (EUD-266)

1147. He knows that in a certain sense the joining of earthly life with beatitude is always an unhappy marriage and that the truly beatific union is concluded only in heaven. (EUD-328)

1148. To want to renounce the world and the world's opinion and then in turn to pay oneself a worldly tribute for having done so is not renunciation of the world. (EUD-374)

1149. . . . Men are not able to conceive of an intelligent man not coveting status and power. (CA-217)

1150. . . . I, after all, am a man of the world, that is, an intelligent but corrupt man. (SOLW-290)

1151. It is in the living room that the battle must be fought, not imaginatively in church . . . Because the victory must be that the home becomes a shrine. (CUP-465)

1152. The Middle Ages made a powerful attempt to think God and the finite together in existence but came to the conclusion that it could not be done, and the expression for the conclusion is the monastery. (CUP-473)

1153. The effect that a person's conception of God or of his eternal happiness should have is that it transforms his entire existence in relation to it, a transformation that is a dying to immediacy. (CUP-483)

1154. Thus cultured people have only a very ironic advantage over simple folk with regard to becoming and continuing to be Christians: the advantage that it is more difficult. (CUP-606)

1155. Just as man's advantage over animals is to be able to live in any climate, so also Christianity's perfection, simply because it is inwardness, is to be able to live, according to its vigor, under the most imperfect conditions and forms, if such be the case. Politics is the external system, this Tantalus-like busyness about external change. (CA-53)

1156. Christianity will not be helped from the outside by institutions and constitutions, and least of all if these are not won through suffering by martyrs in the old-fashioned Christian way but are won in a social and amicable political way, by elections or by a lottery of numbers. (CA-55)

1157. The apostles did not go around talking among themselves, saying: "It is intolerable that the Sanhedrin makes preaching the Word punishable; it is a matter of conscience. What should we do about it? Should we not form a group and send an appeal to the Sanhedrin—or should we take it up at a synodical meeting? It is just possible that by combining with those who otherwise are our enemies we can manage a majority vote so that we can obtain freedom of conscience to proclaim the Word." . . . On the contrary, how did they act?—for no doubt a good many have forgotten. Essentially, "the apostle" is a solitary man. . . . Each one is personally bound to God as a single individual. . . . He lets the established order stand—not a word, not a syllable, not a letter directed toward an external change. . . . "No," says the apostle "just let the established order stand unshakably firm, for by the help of God it also stands unshakably firm that today I am flogged and tomorrow executed or—it amounts to the same thing—that today I proclaim the Word and tomorrow, Amen." Thank you, thank you, that you acted in this way. If you had acted as modern Christians do, Christianity would never have entered the world! (CA-56)

1158. . . . The present age is an age of publicity, the age of miscellaneous announcements: nothing happens but still there is instant publicity. (TA-70)

1159. If someone went around listening to what others said ought to be done and then with a sense of irony . . . did something about it, everybody would be taken aback, would find it rash. (TA-74)

1160. Another danger in reflection is the impossibility of seeing whether it is a resolution reached by deliberation that saves a person from doing evil or whether it is fatigue brought on by deliberation that weakens one and prevents one from doing evil. (TA-77)

1161. An age that is revolutionary but also reflecting and devoid of passion changes the expression of power into a *dialectical tour de force; it lets everything remain but subtly drains the meaning out of it.* (TA-77)

1162. . . . This is *the public.* Only in a passionless but reflective age can this phantom develop with the aid of the press . . . (TA-90)

1163. Only when there is no strong communal life to give substance to the concretion will the press create this abstraction "the public", made up of unsubstantial individuals who are never united or never can be united in the simultaneity of any situation or organization and yet are claimed to be a whole. (TA-91)

1164. Contemporaneity with actual persons, each of whom is someone, in the actuality of the moment and the actual situation gives support to the single individual. But the existence of a public creates no situation and no community. (TA-91)

1165. A generation, a nation, a general assembly, a community, a man still have a responsibility to be something, can know shame for the fickleness and disloyalty, but a public remains the public. . . . The public can become the very opposite and is still the same—the public. (TA-92)

1166. One generation is not better because it understands that a previous generation did wrong, if at the moment it does not itself understand how to distinguish between the views of the moment and of the eternal on the matter! (UDVS-92)

1167. The same people, who as individuals are able to will the good in truth, are immediately corrupted as soon as they unite and become many. (UDVS-96)

1168. . . . The world is more allied with the mediocre than with the truly good . . . (UDVS-98)

1169. The apostle not only reckons the earthly goods as nothing; he even regards them as loss. (UDVS-333)

1170. To make discoveries even with regard to evil, with regard to sin and the multitude of sins, to be the shrewd, sly, foxy, perhaps more or less corrupt observer who can really make discoveries—this is highly regarded in the world. (WOL-283)

1171. "Here lies a world for sale and only awaits a buyer"— provided one does not want to say that the devil has already bought it! (WOL-319)

1172. But money is the world's god; therefore the world thinks that everything that involves money or is connected to money is earnestness. (WOL-320)

1173. An even greater difference, more immense than a difference in language, is the difference between two people, one of whom thinks and speaks only about heavenly things, about God's kingdom and his righteousness, and the other only about a job and livelihood and wife and children, about what is new in the city, and about becoming something in the world. (CD-183)

1174. He no longer belonged to any people; he belonged only to the Lord Jesus. . . . He left [his country] in a way different from that of one who is separated by the ocean from his fatherland; he left it *more inwardly* . . . (CD-184)

1175. . . . On the whole Christianity is suspicious of being honored and esteemed in one's lifetime. (CD-227)

1176. . . . People like very much to keep the essentially Christian at a little distance. (CD-227)

1177. "Woe to you if everyone speaks well of you." Here is not appended "and lies"; it is not necessary, since if everyone speaks well of a person, it must be a lie. (CD-378)

1178. . . . For the secular mentality is nothing more or less than the attribution of infinite worth to the indifferent. (SUD-33)

1179. Is the single individual higher than the established order? (PIC-85)

1180. Strangely enough, this deification of the established order is the perpetual revolt, the continual mutiny against God. (PIC-88)

1181. The deification of the established order is the secularization of everything. . . . The established order wants to be a totality that recognizes nothing above itself but has every individual under it and judges every individual who subordinates himself to the established order . . . (PIC-91)

1182. It does not fear God, it fears people. (PIC-92)

1183. It is, however, untruth, this talk whereby people flatter the human race and themselves that the world is advancing. The world is going neither forward nor backward; it remains essentially the same . . . (PIC-232)

1184. . . . The times are often like a human being—he changes completely but nevertheless remains just as foolish, only in a new pattern—it nevertheless is true that times are different and different times have different requirements. (FSE-15).

1185. Christianity is of the opinion that particularly the true Christian is sober, that on the contrary the less Christian anyone else is the more that person is in a state of intoxication. (JFY-98)

1186. The world *wants* to be deceived; not only is it deceived—ah, then the matter would not be so dangerous!—but it *wants* to be deceived. (JFY-139)

1187. It is just as lunatic as wanting to set up, in the midst of this world, a kingdom that is not of this world. (JFY-175)

1188. He did not steal the rich man's money—no, but he took the idea away from the possession of money. (JFY-177)

1189. It is terrible when blather and grinning threaten to become "public opinion" in a little country. (POV-65)

1190. Take a certain fraction of the good or of the true—this is the sagacious and sensible way to be a success in the world. Take the good or true whole, and the exact opposite occurs and you run completely counter to the world. (POV-242)

1191. When it pleases God in the form of a lowly servant to suffer in this world, the world says, "Poor human being"; when an apostle with a divine commission has the honor to suffer for the truth, the world says, "Poor human being"—poor world! (M-203)

1192. There is nothing to which *God* is so much opposed as hypocrisy—according to God's stipulation, it is precisely life's task to be transformed, since every human being is by nature a born hypocrite. There is nothing *the world* admires as much as the more subtle and the most subtle forms of hypocrisy. (M-302)

1193. All playing at Christianity is recognizable by the partitioning of life so that in practical life, in the actual world, one lets life go the way it is going—and then one is a Christian. What God wanted through Christianity was a transformation of the world, but a transformation of the actual, the practical world. (M-467)

1194. To be *au fait* with the world-view that one's contemporaries admire is always pleasant. (BOA-94)

1195. . . . It undoubtedly is the case that the world at all times has been just about equally good or equally bad. (BOA-227)

1196. Europe as a whole, with mounting momentum of passion, has *worldly* lost its way in problems that can be answered only *divinely*, that only Christianity can answer and—lest anyone be tempted to hail and acclaim what I have to say—has long since answered. (BOA-228)

1197. [Christianity is] the kingdom that at no price wants to be a kingdom of this world. (M-55)

Newspapers and Journalism

1198. When, namely, one wants to put some nonsense in a character's mouth, for the creative writer . . . it can be achieved in two ways, either—by virtue of reason and with its superiority—one looks down into the foggy realm of nonsense, or one takes something one does not understand and silently draws the conclusion: When I do not understand it, it is nonsense. (I say "silently," for it is not always advisable to hint this aloud), and thereupon copies or rather draws it, which, of course those who have to copy anything they do not understand must always do. (EPW-221)

1199. To print a rumor does not make it more true . . . (CA-156)

1200. In everyday life, protest is promptly made and rules and regulations and preventive measures are immediately devised when the drinking water in the city is polluted or the baker uses contaminated flour, or even when the streetlights do not burn. But when polluted and contaminated food is offered for sale in the world of the spirit, when there seems to be an enormous customer demand . . . then nothing happens. (CA-166)

1201. [In the case of a servant complaining to the newspaper of bring wronged by his master] Here no mitigating words of admonition are heard, here the injured party is not initiated into any uplifting view of life that could teach him to bear a wrong with true human pride in humility before God. No, revenge, revenge . . . . Which, then, is worse—the sickness or the remedy! And what is the relation between the alleged protest of a misuse of power and the irreparable harm done by the misuse of impotence. (CA-167)

1202. As stated, the alehouse keeper reads *The Corsair*. He believes that what appears in the newspapers is public opinion, the voice of the people and of truth. (CA-180)

1203. It is a matter of common knowledge that a trifle, a nothing, creates the biggest sensation and especially gossip. (CA-197)

1204. I am no fool who believes that the world becomes better because it praises me or, worse, because it censures me . . . (CA-202)

1205. It is the press that actually destroys all personality. That a cowardly wretch can sit in hiding and write and print for the thousands! All personal conduct and all personal power must run aground on this. (CA-218)

1206. With the press as degenerate as it is, human beings eventually will surely be transformed into clods. A newspaper's first concern has to be circulation; from then on, the rule for what it publishes can be: the wittiness and entertainment of printing something without any relation to communication through the press. How significant! How easy to be witty when misuse of the press had become the newly invented kind of witticism . . . The lunatic press thrives. (CA-220)

1207.   . . . On the whole the press, representing abstract, impersonal communication, is demoralizing, especially since the daily press, purely formally and with no regard to whether what it says is true or false, contributes enormously to demoralization because of all the impersonality, which in turn is more or less irresponsibility and impenitence, that anonymity, the highest expression for abstraction, impersonality, impenitence and irresponsibility, is a basic source of modern demoralization . . . (POV-57)

1208.   But in our day, when that which is the secret of evil has become wisdom—namely, that one is not to ask about the communicator but only about the communication . . . (POV-57)

1209.   The daily press is the state's disaster, "the crowd" the world's evil. (POV-168)

1210.   One becomes so accustomed to hearing all this about the age as an age of movement, that the times demand one thing today, tomorrow the opposite, that a brand new system is imminent—one becomes so accustomed to hearing this that it makes no more impression on one than cursing makes an impression on a sailor. One becomes as accustomed to the vortex of the newspapers as to evening prayers. . . . One becomes so accustomed to it that one falls asleep reading it. (M-384)

1211. The press is often guilty of a *petitio principii* in its tactics; it pretends to be *reporting* a *factual* state and *aims* to *produce* it. (M-386)

1212. In civil life, as far as I now, it is forbidden under penalty of the law to raise an untruthful hue and cry; in literature we are thrown to the wolves, all we poor wretches who do not publish a newspaper every evening. (M-387)

1213. . . . A journalist has a suprahuman voice by which he drowns out all others, and he does this every evening. Previously the world has seen despot tyranny, money tyranny, mental tyranny—but yelling tyranny is the most recent; it is journalism's. (M-388)

1214. According to our contemporary way of thinking one would have expected that the Lord would at least have waited to let himself be born until the art of printing had been invented, that until then the fullness of time had not arrived . . . (D-24)

1215. The journalist makes people ridiculous in two ways. First, by making them believe it is necessary to have an opinion. . . . Secondly, by hiring out an opinion . . . (D-69)

1216. The demoralization which comes from the press can be seen from this fact: There are not ten men in every generation who, socratically, are afraid of having a wrong opinion; but there are thousands and millions who are more frightened of standing alone, even with an opinion which is quite right, than of anything else. But when something is in the papers, it is *eo ipso* certain that there is always a good number of people having that opinion or about to express it. *Journals* (KA-430)

1217. Indeed, if the press were to hang a sign out like every other trade, it would have to read: Here men are demoralized in the shortest possible time on the largest possible scale for the smallest possible price. *Journals* (KA-431)

1218. What we need is a Pythagorean silence. There is a far greater need for total-abstaining societies which would not read newspapers than for ones which do not drink alcohol. *Journals* (KA-431)

1219. The lowest depth to which people can sink before God is defined by the word "Journalist." . . . If I were a father and had a daughter who was seduced, I should not despair over her; I would hope for her salvation. But if I had a son who became a journalist, and continued to be one for five years, I would give him up . . . *Journals* (KA-431)

Deception

1220. Talleyrand's famous statement that man did not acquire speech in order to reveal his thoughts but in order to conceal them. . . . [the world wants to be deceived; therefore let it be deceived] (COI-253)

1221. . . . But the person who deceives himself is continually deceived even if he flees to the farthest limits of the world, because he cannot escape himself. (EUD-211)

1222. The most dangerously deceived person is the one who is self-deceived, the most dangerous condition is that of the one who is deceived by much knowledge . . . (TDIO-35)

1223. Zealousness to learn from life is seldom found, but all the more frequently a desire, inclination, and reciprocal haste to be deceived by life. (TA-10)

1224. . . . There is an ignorance of oneself that is just as lamentable for the learned one and the simple one, both of whom are bound in the same responsibility: this ignorance is called self-deception. (UDVS-23)

1225. . . . There are also sleepy souls who not only call it pleasant but even upbuilding to be lulled to sleep. (UDVS-31)

1226. It is terrible to see a person seek solace by plunging into the vortex of despair, but even more terrible is the composure that in the anguish of death a person does not call out in a scream for help . . . but calmly wants to be a witness to his own perdition. (UDVS-33)

1227. We can be deceived by believing what is untrue, but we certainly are also deceived by not believing what is true. . . . Whose recovery is more doubtful, that of the one who does not see, or that of the person who sees and yet does not see? (WOL-5)

1228. The tree is known by its *fruits*. It is true that the tree is also known by its *leaves*, but the fruit is still the essential mark. Thus if you identified a tree by its leaves to be such and such a tree but in the fruit season discovered that it bore no fruit, you would then know that it was not the tree that according to the leaves it purported to be. (WOL-11)

1229. In the infinite sense, only one deception is possible— self-deception. (WOL-235)

1230. Most of what people of this kind say about believing in God and feeling God close to them is simply illusion, an intensified self-esteem and sense of vitality that they confuse with religiousness. They believe themselves to be, as they say, the object of the fatherly care of providence. Ultimately it is nothing more nor less than a sense of coziness in life. (WOL-473)

1231. And is it not the case that the older a person grows, the more and more of a swindle life proves to be, that the smarter he becomes and the more ways he learns to shift for himself, the bigger the mess he makes of life and the more he suffers! (R-172)

1232. But there is also another kind of hypocrisy, hypocrites who resemble the Pharisee but have chosen the tax collector as their prototype. . . . "God, I thank you that I am not like this tax collector," sanctimoniously say, "God, I thank you that I am not like this Pharisee." (WA-127)

1233. . . . If a man is presumably happy, imagines himself to be happy, although considered in the light of truth he is unhappy, he is usually far from wanting to be wrenched out of his error. (SUD-43)

1234. . . . Illusion essentially has two forms: the illusion of hope and the illusion of recollection. Youth has the illusion of hope; he has this illusion, he also has the utterly biased idea of illusion that there is only the illusion of hope. . . . This *fuimus* [we have been], which is common to older people, is just as great an illusion as the illusions of young people about the future: they both lie or fictionalize. (SUD-58)

1235. There is always a secular mentality that no doubt wants to have the name of being Christian but wants to become Christian as cheaply as possible. (FSE-16)

1236. What this age has invented is untruth, that it is number (the numerical), the crowd, or the most honored and most honored cultured public from which reformations proceed. (FSE-19)

1237. . . . How true it is that the world wants to be deceived. (JFY-91)

1238. The world, as is natural, speaks about this world, simply and solely about this world, does not know and does not wish to know that there is another world . . . (JFY-150)

Language and Precise Expression

1239. They do indeed know how to speak but do not know how to converse. (COI-33)

1240. . . . There is a resemblance to conversation only because they do not all talk at once. (COI-34)

1241. Lessing [the poet] has already wittily distinguished between replying to a question and answering it . . . (COI-35)

1242. . . . One can ask without any interest in the answer . . . (COI-36)

1243. Now, truth demands identity, for if I had the thought without the word, then I would not have the thought; and if I had the word without the thought, then I would not have the word, either—just as one cannot say of children and deranged people that they speak. (COI-247)

1244. Which medium is abstract? . . . It is the medium that is furthest removed from language. (E/O I-56)

1245. . . . Incomprehensible—incomprehensible. . . . Said about God, this signifies the highest; when one is obliged to say it about a human being, it always signifies a defect, at times a sin. (E/O II-14)

1246. To be sure a poet [Lessing] has rightly said that a sigh to God without words is the best worship. . . . But if God is to be present to the soul, then the sigh presumably finds the thought, and the thought presumably the words . . . (TDIO-16)

1247. . . . Clarity, even if it has no desire to disturb anything, demands the word to the very end. (TDIO-43)

1248. Yet how rich is language in the service of desire in comparison with language when it describes actuality. (SOLW-29)

1249. . . . Copiousness of thought is not always proportionate to copiousness of words. (CUP-42)

1250. . . . Talleyrand's well-known saying: Man has received language in order to conceal his thoughts. (CA-79)

1251. In the same way we are willing to keep Christian terminology but privately know that nothing decisive is supposed to be meant by it. (TA-81)

1252. But because the ability to speak is an advantage, it does not follow that the ability to be silent would not be an art or would be an inferior art. On the contrary, because the human being is able to speak, the ability to be silent is an art, and a great art precisely because this advantage of his so easily tempts him. (WA-10)

1253. The advantage of the human being over the animal is the ability to speak, but, in relation to God, wanting to speak can easily become the corruption of the human being, who is able to speak. (WA-11)

1254. . . . It is very important for a person that his language be precise and true, because that means his thinking is that also. (PIC-158)

1255. . . . There is also an art of eloquence that comes from evil . . . (FSE-11)

1256. That he has burned his Hegelian manuscripts makes
no difference whatever, because, since he has not taken
the time to acquire proficiency in the language of Christian concepts, the consequence is quite simple, that he
has nothing at all to hold on to if burning the manuscripts was really identical with renouncing this philosophy . . . (BOA-111)

1257. In other words, emotion that is Christian is controlled
by conceptual definitions . . . (BOA-112)

1258. . . . Pagan views, pagan conceptions of God, can be expressed in deep emotion. In order to be able to express
oneself Christianly, proficiency and schooling in the
Christian conceptual definitions are also required in
addition to the more universal heart language of deep
emotion . . . (BOA-113)

1259. But if one starts with the premise that the essentially
Christian is something vague and indefinite, well, then
one can easily meditate. (BOA-115)

1260. The essentially Christian exists before any Christian exists; it must exist in order for one to become a Christian. (BOA-117)

1261. If the essentially Christian enters into the hearts of ever
so many believers, every believer realizes that it did not
arise in his heart. Realizes that the objective qualification of the essentially Christian is not reminiscence as
erotic love is of falling in love. (BOA-118)

1262. The confusion is continually due to Magister Adler's not having respect for or mastery of Christian conceptual language. (BOA-123)

1263. Profundity is related to coherence and continuity. (BOA-283)

XII. MISCELLANEOUS QUOTATIONS

Aphorisms and Observations

1264. When [The Copenhagen Post] was on its way to bankruptcy, it did as all bankrupt people do: it lived luxuriously . . . (EPW-26)

1265. . . . Life is not something abstract but something extremely individual. (EPW-47)

1266. . . . Natural development does not proceed by leaps . . . (EPW-47)

1267. . . . The endless calculating of the circumstances of pleasure impedes and stifles pleasure itself. (COI-61)

1268. [Socrates] had come not to save the world but to judge it. His life was dedicated to that . . . (COI-173)

1269. No matter how strong a person is, no person is stronger than himself. (EUD-18)

1270. . . . The highest cannot be bought at too high a price. (EUD-379)

1271. . . . It nevertheless remains certain that anyone who buys from God will never be deceived by having his purchase later prove to be of lesser worth. (EUD-398)

1272. He alone is truly happy who is not deluded into thinking that the repetition should be something new, for then one grows weary of it. (R-132)

1273. Who could want to be susceptible to every fleeting thing, the novel, which always enervatingly diverts the soul anew? (R-133)

1274. It is often distressing to be an observer—it has the same melancholy effect as being a police officer. (R-135)

1275. In relation to a girl, one should be chivalrous enough not merely to be oneself but also to be the prosecuting attorney on her behalf. (R-191)

1276. . . . For it never fails that one fool going his way takes several others along with him. (PF-12)

1277. . . . Trying to get rid of something by sleeping is just as useless as trying to obtain something by sleeping. (PF-43)

1278. Philosophy begins with wonder . . . (PF-143)

1279. One does not start out on a journey around the world in the same way one starts out for a stroll. (PF-163)

1280. . . . A completely indifferent will is an absurdity and a chimera. (COA-viii)

1281. . . . The solution of doubt lies not in reflection but in resolution. (COA-ix)

1282. When the understanding takes to the mythical, the outcome is seldom more than small talk. (COA-32)

1283. . . . Anxiety is the dizziness of freedom. (COA-56)

1284. . . . The older and the more spiritually developed the individuality is, the less beautiful it is in sleep, whereas the child is more beautiful in sleep. (COA-65)

1285. . . . Anxiety is defined as freedom's disclosure to itself in possibility. (COA-111)

1286. If an observer will only pay attention to himself, he will have enough with five men, five women, and ten children for the discovery of all possible states of the human soul. (COA-126)

1287. Mockery is the highest and apparently the freest expression of unbelief. (COA-140)

1288. There is an old saying that to understand and to understand are two things. To understand a speech is one thing, and to understand what it refers to, namely, the personal, is something else. (COA-142)

1289. Aristotle's view [was] that philosophy begins with wonder, not as in our day with doubt . . . (COA-175)

1290. . . . Even if I debate with the devil himself, I cannot debate with my wife. (P-7)

1291.   . . . The sound of a crowd affects a speaker as martial music does, as the whistle of the bowstring affects the warrior. (P-27)

1292.   The category "all" makes no petty distinction; it includes all. (P-55)

1293.   . . . Truth is the criterion of itself and of the false. (P-57)

1294.   But religious debauchery is still the most dreadful of all. (TDIO-35)

1295.   . . . What is all eloquence but deceit! (TDIO-49)

1296.   Indeed, to be a good reader or a good listener is just as great as to be a speaker . . . (TDIO-58)

1297.   . . . The world never seems to be short of guides. (TDIO-60)

1298.   . . . Death is the only certainty . . . (TDIO-75)

1299.   . . . The multitude of the dead do not form any kind of society. (TDIO-89)

1300.   . . . Just as nature declares God, so every grave preaches. (TDIO-109)

1301.   Remembrance of the God-fearing is a benediction. (TDIO-112)

1302.   When someone starts out on a long journey, we wish him good fortune—but the few steps up to the altar . . .? And yet it is the most dangerous journey. (TDIO-113)

1303. I consider being a good listener just as great as being a good speaker, and perhaps at times the former is even the greater . . . (TDIO-120)

1304. When an ape looks in, no apostle can look out. (SOLW-8)

1305. In sawing wood, one should not press down too hard on the saw; . . . the speculative thinker should make himself objectively light . . . (CUP-57)

1306. . . . He was not a speaker but a bellows pumper. (CUP-146)

1307. . . . He will be finished with before life is finished with him. (CUP-163)

1308. It [demonstrating immortality] is like wanting to paint Mars in the armor that makes him invisible. (CUP-174)

1309. Mood is like the Niger River in Africa; no one knows its source, no one knows its outlet—only its reach is known! (CUP-237)

1310. But eternity sentences forever the very first time. (CUP-533)

1311. Direct recognizability is paganism. (CUP-599)

1312. The first requirement for a singer is voice. . . . The ability to infuse voice with imagination, to be able to sing with imagination. (CA-29)

1313. . . . One ought not challenge the gods with foolish wishes lest they mock one—not by denying the wish but by fulfilling it. (CA-48)

1314. There is no poet without madness. (CA-73)

1315. . . . That to which I give the most thought I always understand far better afterwards . . . (CA-208)

1316. . . . It is the religious that redeems. (CA-211)

1317. . . . To be torn to death by *envy* is also a slow way to die. (CA-220)

1318. . . . It is easy for a young man to have a tranquil mind; he does not know the world. (CA-165)

1319. . . . Perhaps the most dangerous temptations are those that come under the modest label of "nothing at all." (CA-180)

1320. . . . The voice of God is always a whisper . . . (TA-10)

1321. Entrapped air always becomes noxious, and the entrapment of reflection with no ventilating action or event develops censorious envy. (TA-82)

1322. Envy in the process of *establishing* itself takes the form of *leveling* . . . (TA-84)

1323. . . . Inspired words are quickly forgotten in the trivialities of life . . . (UDVS-31)

1324.   . . . One who craves becomes like that which he craves. (UDVS-34)

1325.   Alas, time and busyness think that eternity is very far away . . . (UDVS-66)

1326.   A mirror, it is true, has the feature that a person can see his image in it, but then one must stand still. If one hastily hurries by, one gets to see nothing. (UDVS-67)

1327.   Yes, the sun does not shine more equally upon the peasant's hut and the ruler's palace than the eternal looks equally upon the highest and the lowliest . . . (UDVS-81)

1328.   Dependence on God is the only independence . . . (UDVS-182)

1329.   . . . Some wear the medal to their honor and others honor the medal by wearing it. (UDVS-199)

1330.   But living for the eternal begins with seeking God's kingdom first. (UDVS-209)

1331.   . . . The most dangerous slavery [is] the small-minded fear of people who are one's equals. (UDVS-326)

1332.   Only the eternal can be and become and remain contemporary with every age. (WOL-31)

1333.   . . . Despair is the lack of the eternal. (WOL-41)

1334.   If anyone thinks that by falling in love or by finding a friend a person has learned Christian love, he is in profound error. (WOL-57)

1335. . . . And yet loving each one individually but no one exceptionally. (WOL-67)

1336. Thus the one who actually occupies himself with the eternal is never busy. (WOL-98)

1337. . . . In relation to God, every person begins with an infinite debt . . . (WOL-102)

1338. Does it not amount to the same thing: to see a mirage—and not to see? (WOL-162)

1339. Take someone who is infinitely superior to others in understanding, and you will see that he appears to be a simple soul. (WOL-242)

1340. Mercifulness is how it is given. (WOL-327)

1341. . . . So that a person can no more bully his way into God's kingdom than he can cowardly and spinelessly whimper his way in. (WOL-406)

1342. . . . No one is ever innocent in being presumptuous . . . (CD-60)

1343. Being lovely without the knowledge that disfigures loveliness. (CD-62)

1344. Is it not true . . . that the person who lives on his old place but far from his only wish nevertheless lives at a distance? (CD-63)

1345. The one who wants an end must also want the means. (CD-95)

1346. . . . A human being scarcely has the slightest idea of how scrupulous God can be. (CD-295)

1347. . . . In order to *represent* Juliet an actress must essentially have a distance in age from Juliet. (CD-321)

1348. . . . There is something accidental in every genuine love affair. (CD-329)

1349. . . . God's Kingdom can be sought only if it is sought first . . . (WA-18)

1350. . . . Where God is the schoolmaster all the children labor more or less under the delusion that they are big, grown-up people . . . (WA-31)

1351. . . . No one teaches joy better than one who is joyful oneself. (WA-36)

1352. . . . Simplicity is that the teacher himself is what he is teaching. (WA-37)

1353. To honor one's father because he is exceptionally intelligent is impiety. (WA-101)

1354. He who laughs last laughs best, but in truth he also conquers best who conquers last . . . (WA-214)

1355. . . . He who does not have a God does not have a self either. (SUD-40)

1356. . . . For the old legend about breaking a certain magic spell is true; the piece has to be played thorough backwards or the spell is not broken. (SUD-44)

1357. . . . The self must be broken in order to become itself, but quit despairing over that. (SUD-65)

1358. . . . A believer, after all, is a lover . . . (SUD-103)

1359. From men, man learns to speak, from the gods, to be silent. (SUD-127)

1360. . . . To be neutral about Christ is offense. (SUD-129)

1361. The helper [Christ] is the help. (PIC-15)

1362. No, if there is something you want to forget, then try to find something else to remember. (PIC-152)

1363. . . . Flesh and blood and self-love are very sly. (FSE-36)

1364. . . . If one is reminded every day to forget, one never does really forget. (FSE-37)

1365. But silence brought into a house—that is eternity's art of making a house a home. (FSE-50)

1366. That [declaring Jesus insane] would be just as foolish, it is generally agreed, as for ants to think they could get rid of the anteater's tongue by declaring it insane. (JFY-176)

1367. . . . Silence can also be an untruth . . . (POV-89)

1368. . . . *The single individual* is and remains the fixed point that can hold against pantheistic confusion . . . (POV-123)

1369. Piety at rest is Jewish piety; a militant piety . . . is Christianity or being a Christian. (POV-130)

1370. He will be just like that hero who himself gave the firing orders at his own execution. (POV-281)

1371. . . . An eternal happiness is a priceless good . . . (M-64)

1372. What Christianity needs is not the suffocating protection of the state; no, it needs fresh air, persecution, and— God's protection. (M-158)

1373. So it is religiously. The most corrupting of all is to satisfy what is not yet a need. (M-159)

1374. . . . God is a power against whom one cannot rebel in defiance. (M-190)

1375. . . . According to the New Testament one must be an adult in order to be able to become a Christian. (M-237)

1376. Imagine the futility of wanting to be at odds with an eternal changelessness . . . (M-278)

1377. . . . Of all deceivers, fear most yourself! (M-297)

1378. . . . How terrible to deceive oneself eternally! (M-300)

1379. There is nothing to which *God* is so much opposed as hypocrisy . . . (M-302)

1380. . . . To give in the slightest with regard to principles is to give them up, and to give up one's principles is to give up oneself. (M-319)

1381. Existence is acoustic. Just pay attention to what the re-joinder replies and you will immediately know which is which. (M-334)

1382. . . . Any lack of character pleases this world. (M-335)

1383. Christianity is a gift, if you will, stipulated for human-ity according to the testament of the Savior of the world. But there is a responsibility . . . the gift and the re-sponsibility correspond to each other altogether equally . . . the responsibility is: the imitation of Jesus Christ. (M-336)

1384. But when the right man comes, yes, then is the mo-ment. (M-338)

1385. The most glorious powers are set in motion in order to get a committee set up; as soon as it is done, no one cares about the matter anymore. (M-389)

1386. Descartes correctly says somewhere that nothing great ever came out of an association. (M-390)

1387. . . . There is a finite self-love in all finite power. (M-391)

1388. What people want in fact is the most convenient reli-gion possible . . . (M-453)

1389. A Christian is a person who has caught on fire. (M-465)

1390. . . . God is not impressed by millions. (M-471)

1391. . . . There is a stoppage that, spiritually understood, is what constipation is in the animal organism . . . (BOA-9)

1392. The essential author is essentially a teacher . . . (BOA-15)

1393. He consumes, because he communicates doubt. (BOA-15)

1394. One rarely manages to get a scholarly blatherpate, who basically knows nothing, to become involved in anything concrete. (BOA-146)

1395. The way in which victory is won is just as important as the victory. (BOA-255)

1396. Indeterminableness is the basis of dizziness. . . . Therefore the remedy for dizziness is limitation; and in the spiritual sense all discipline is limitation. (BOA-288)

1397. . . . It may be true as the proverb says: *variato delectat* [change pleases], but in the world of the spirit continuity is not only joy but is spirit itself . . . (BOA-300)

1398. It is unthinkable that it could occur to a human being who has reached a conclusion about himself as a spirit in relation to eternity, to choose physical science (with its empirical material) as a field for his efforts. (D-98)

1399. If Christ had known about the microscope, he would have examined the apostles before accepting them. (D-99)

1400. The secret of life, if one wants to get on well, is: plenty of chitchat about what one intends to do and how one is kept from doing it—and no action. (D-108)

1401. . . . It pleases the world that there are some who are worse than the average. (D-116)

1402. What ability there is in an individual may be measured by the yardstick of how far there is between his *understanding* and his *will*. (D-126)

1403. . . . The Highest, after all, is not to *comprehend* the Highest, but to do it. (D-146)

1404. Mysticism has not the patience to wait for God's revelation. *Journal* Sept 6, 1839 (KA-12)

1405. . . . The reason why I far prefer the autumn to the spring is because in the autumn one looks up to heaven—in spring at the earth. *Journal* Oct 7, 1837 (KA-10)

1406. People nowadays go to church to be entertained and to the theatre to be edified. Repetition (KA 146)

Anecdotes

1407. Anyone who wants to harvest before he sows or as soon as he has sown, anyone who wants to be victorious without struggling, anyone who wants something but does not want the means is a fool in people's eyes. (EUD-213)

1408. On the battlefield, it so happens that if the first line of combatants has been victorious, then the second is not led into battle at all but merely shares in the triumph. In the world of the spirit, it is not this way. (EUD-394)

1409. But according to Socrates the unity of virtue [there is one form of excellence; the forms of evil are infinite] is like a tyrant who does not have the courage to rule over the actual world but first murders all his subjects in order to be able to rule proudly and with perfect security over the silent kingdom of pale shadows. (COI-58)

1410. . . . Our generation does not stop with faith, does not stop with the miracle of faith, turning water into wine— it goes further and turns wine into water. (FAT-37)

1411. Fools and young people say that everything is possible for a human being. But that is a gross error. Spiritually speaking, everything is possible, but in the finite world there is much that is not possible. (FAT-44)

1412. Was Job proved to be in the wrong? Yes, eternally, for there is no higher court than the one that judged him. Was Job proved to be in the right? Yes, eternally, by being proved to be in the wrong *before God*. (R-212)

1413. The physician would promise to issue a report as soon as possible, along with a tabulated statistical survey in order to determine the average. And when one has arrived at the average, everything is explained. (COA-122)

1414. Hegel, on the contrary, despite all his outstanding ability and stupendous learning, reminds us again and again by his performance that he was in the German sense a professor of philosophy on a large scale, because he *à tout prix* (at any price) must explain all things. (COA-20)

1415. . . . While it is beautiful to listen to a brook running murmuring through life, it is nevertheless comical that a sum of rational creatures is transformed into a perpetual muttering without meaning. (COA-94)

1416. Who does not know that talkative barber, the tale of whose journey was in inverse relation to his journey, which was only very short . . . (P-103)

1417. What I am concerned with is something else; it is the transmission of sound through the medium that is called the crowd and that may also be called gossip. Here one will run across oddities of the most amazing sort; there occurs what is otherwise unheard of, that sound transmits itself in such a way that when one says one thing it becomes in transmission, something entirely different—the only instance in which transmission departs from the rule: to produce something resembling itself. (P-138)

1418. Long live autumn! There is only one glass of the champagne worth drinking, only one piece of the roast worth eating, at only one time is a girl worth loving, and there is only one girl worth this one time—and only autumn *is the season of the year. . . . Autumn is the Time of Colors.* (P-156)

1419. Similarly Hegel also is supposed to have died with the words that no one understood him except one person, who misunderstood him . . . (CUP-70)

1420. When commission agent Behrend had lost a silk umbrella, he advertised for a cotton umbrella, because he thought this way: If I say that it is a silk umbrella, the finder will be more easily tempted to keep it. (CUP-108)

1421. Having to exist with the help of the guidance of pure thinking is like having to travel in Denmark with a small map of Europe on which Denmark is no larger than a steel pen-point—indeed, even more impossible. (CUP-310)

1422. From the ethical point of view, actuality is superior to possibility. . . . The ethical immediately embraces the single individual. . . . It does not bluster about millions and generations; it does not take humankind at random, any more than the police arrest humankind in general. (CUP-320)

1423. . . . An aristocratic landed proprietor, goes to church for the sake of his servants in order to set them a good example—of how not to go to church. (CUP-511)

1424. Many grieved at Socrates' death sentence, but Xanthippe was strident and said: How can it be that an innocent man should suffer this. Socrates answered: Would you rather have me guilty?" (CA-161)

1425. In small rooms, care must be taken to air out once in a while; care must be taken to keep the water clean in a small reservoir, a precaution not at all necessary if the reservoir is the sea. (CA-204)

1426.   . . . Ennoblement by means of depravity is like the no-
        bility of a man who cannot get along without money,
        acquires his wealth unlawfully, and then uses it to do
        considerable good. (TA-40)

1427.   In Germany there are even handbooks for lovers; so it
        probably will end with lovers being able to sit and speak
        anonymously to each other. (TA-104)

1428.   When a woman works on a cloth for sacred use . . .
        [and] the cloth is finished . . . then she is deeply dis-
        tressed if anyone were to make the mistake of seeing
        her artistry instead of the meaning of the cloth or were
        to make the mistake of seeing a defect instead of seeing
        the meaning of the cloth. (UDVS-5)

1429.   But the danger is that the person in love and the enthu-
        siast take a wrong turn and swing off to the great in-
        stead of being led to the good. It is certain that the good
        is truly the great, but the great is not always the good.
        (UDVS-35)

1430.   It is certain that ordinarily a person acts more sensibly,
        shows more energy, apparently more self-control, when
        others are watching him than when he believes himself
        unobserved. (UDVS-53)

1431.   Temporality's comfort is a dubious matter, because it
        lets the wound close although it is not healed, and yet
        the physician knows that recovery comes through keep-
        ing the wound open. (UDVS-100)

1432.   Or if there were two girls, and the one said to her be-
        loved, "You will come again tomorrow, won't you?" and

the other said, "Oh thank you for coming today"—which of the two would be more convinced that the beloved would come again tomorrow? (UDVS-180)

1433. If you do to people what is right and just forget God, are you then practicing righteousness? Is not practicing righteousness in this way like the thief's doing what is right and just with the money he has stolen? (UDVS-211)

1434. . . . If you imagine a young man standing on the threshold of his life, where many roads lie open before him, and asking himself which career he would like to follow, is it not true that he would make careful inquiries into where each particular road lead or, what amounts to the same thing, try to find out who has walked this road previously (UDVS-225)

1435. Does not the presence of a king make one speak differently: Your Majesty, it is a trifling matter. In the presence of the beloved, we speak differently: Darling it is a small matter. (UDVS-315)

1436. The adage has it that a pound of gold and a pound of feathers weigh the same . . . but . . . two magnitudes cannot be weighed together. Why not? Because the scale cannot indicate that the one pound is gold and the other pound feathers. The distinction is not between happiness and suffering, but between *eternal* happiness and *temporal* suffering. (UDVS-318)

1437. Concerning spiritual matters, one cannot, if one wishes to avoid speaking foolishly, talk like a shopkeeper who carries the best grade of goods but in addition has a medium grade, which he can also very well recommend as almost as good. (WOL-45)

1438. In the business world it is more common that a firm fails because suddenly in a single stroke too great a demand is made upon it, but in the world of spirit it is the duration that does away with so many. (WOL-309)

1439. *When.* The superior force had haughtily announced what its countless troops would do when they had conquered everything; the terse reply was "*When.*" (CD-190)

1440. . . . The great difficulty bound up with being an idol is that it is almost inconceivable that one can receive honorable discharge from this appointment. (CD-304)

1441. Everything essentially Christian must have in its presentation a resemblance to the way a physician speaks at the sickbed; even if only medical experts understand it, it must never be forgotten that the situation is the bedside of a sick person. (SUD-5)

1442. But sin grows every moment that one does not take leave of it. . . . There is even a proverb that says to sin is human but to remain in sin is of the devil. (SUD-106)

1443. The superior person understands, and the more truly superior the more concerned in responsibility he understands, what will benefit the other and then wants to do everything to benefit him—and then perceives with sadness that the other understands neither himself nor him. (PIC-71)

1444. The question is just as foolish, just exactly as foolish, as if someone were to ask a man with whom he was standing and talking, "May I put this question to you, do you exist?" (PIC-204)

1445. . . . The story of that actor of old who was so able to enter into emotions that he even wept when he came home from the theater and wept for several days. (FSE-18)

1446. There is a story about a traveler who was short of money out in the country although he did indeed have a large denomination bank note—there was no one who could change it. So also with Christianity and the disciple. (JFY-162)

1447. One ought, however, always to watch this category "approximation" a little so that it is not made so broad as to include those whose—Christianity!—is a distancing from Christianity. When on the way to town one meets someone, it is very easy to make a mistake momentarily and not notice whether he is going to or coming from town. (JFY-209)

1448. Naturally it will cost money, since without money one gets nothing in this world, not even a certificate for becoming eternally happy in the next world. (M-109)

1449. As is well known, Heiberg's Councilor Herr Zierlich is so sensitive to propriety that he even finds it improper for women's and men's clothing to hang together in a wardrobe. (M-162)

1450. Nothing is easier for the one providing the corrective than to add the other side; but then it ceases to be precisely the corrective and itself becomes an established order. (M-403)

1451. To be salt means not to exist for oneself but to exist for others, that is, to be sacrificed. *Salt* has no being in itself but is purely teleological, and to be qualified wholly in a teleological way means to be sacrificed. (M-452)

1452. What money is in the finite world, concepts are in the world of spirit. All transactions are conducted with them. (M-463)

1453. . . . It is only quite figuratively that the soldier can be called courageous who courageously advances against the enemy because behind him stands a man with a loaded gun who shoots him down if he does not—courageously advance against the enemy. (M-489)

1454. . . . Wanting only to sound the alarm, wanting only to prompt a discussion, is not very praiseworthy if the experience [is] repeated again and again. (BOA-12)

1455. Just as it is told of those two princely personages who were so very obese that they exercised by walking around each other . . . (BOA-27)

1456. There are examples of people who, embarrassed and embarrassing, continue sitting with one for whole hours just because they feel embarrassed about leaving (BOA-273)

1457. The sophist thought, and all obtuse people are of the same opinion, that the more he talked the more he manifested his wisdom. (BOA-284)

1458. To me he seems like a child who is so delighted at being able to do a trick that he keeps on doing it and cannot get it into his head that there very likely are others who are able to do it. (BOA-285)

1459. A few years ago I heard a parson deliver on two successive Sundays exactly the same discourse . . . At a court reception when the Queen had told a story, and all the courtiers had laughed, including a deaf minister, who then arose and craved permission to tell his story—and told the same one—the question is, what was his view of the significance of repetition? *Repetition* (KA-137)

1460. For you can become accustomed to the thunder of a hundred cannon, so that you can sit at table and hear the most insignificant remark more clearly than the roar of the hundred cannon you are in the habit of hearing. . . . No, only the "thou shalt" of eternity—and the listening ear which will hear this "thou shalt"—can save you from the thralldom of habit. *Works of Love* (KA-300)

1461. If the natural sciences had been developed in Socrates' day as they are now, all the sophists would have been scientists. One would have hung a microscope outside his shop in order to attract custom, and then would have had a sign painted saying: "Learn and see through a giant microscope how a man thinks" (and on reading the advertisement Socrates would have said: "That is how men who do not think behave"). *Journals* (KA-430)

Parables

1462. **The Theater, the Clown and the Fire**
In a theater, it happened that a fire started offstage. The clown came out to tell the audience. They thought it was a joke and applauded. He told them again, and they became still more hilarious. This is the way, I suppose, that the world will be destroyed—amid the universal hilarity of wits and wags who think it is all a joke. (E/O I-30)

1463. **The Jinni**
If I had in my service a submissive jinni who, when I asked for a glass of water, would bring me the world's most expensive wines, deliciously blended, in a goblet, I would dismiss him until he learned that the enjoyment consists not in what I enjoy but in getting my own way. (E/O I-31)

1464. **The Conqueror and the Possessor**
. . . If I imagine a conqueror who subjugated kingdoms and countries, he would indeed possess these subjugated provinces, he would have great possessions, and yet one would call such a prince a conquering and not a possessing prince. Only when he guided these countries with wisdom to what was best for them, only then would he possess them. . . . To conquer takes pride, to possess takes humility; to conquer takes violence, to possess, patience; to conquer—greed, to possess—contentment with little; to conquer requires eating and drinking, to possess, prayer and fasting. (E/O II-131)

1465. **The Cup**
I shall look up to this umpire, I shall covet his approval even though I cannot deserve it. And when the cup of suffering is handed to me, I shall not fix my gaze upon the cup but upon the one who hands it to me, and I shall not stare at the bottom of the cup to see whether I have quickly emptied it but steadfastly at the one who hands it to me. I shall gladly take the cup in my hand; I shall not empty it to somebody else's health as on a festive occasion when I myself delight in the delicious drink. No, I shall taste its bitterness, and while I am tasting it I shall cry out to myself "to *my* health," because I know and am convinced that with this drink I am acquiring by purchase an eternal health. (E/O II-287)

1466. **Guidance for the Future**
How, then, should we face the future? When the sailor is out on the ocean, when everything is changing all around him, when the waves are born and die, he does not stare down into the waves, because they are changing. He looks up at the stars. Why? Because they are faithful; they have the same location now that they had for our ancestors and will have for generations to come. By what means does he conquer the changeable? By the eternal. (EUD-19)

1467. **Reflecting God's Likeness**
Only when he himself becomes nothing, only then can God illuminate him so that he resembles God. However great he is, he cannot manifest God's likeness; God can imprint himself in him only when he himself has become nothing. When the ocean is exerting all its power, that is precisely the time when it cannot reflect

the image of heaven, and even the slightest motion blurs the image; but when it becomes still and deep, the image of heaven sinks into its nothingness. (EUD-399)

1468. Abraham, the Religious Man

Abraham is an eternal prototype of the religious man. Just as he had to leave the land of his fathers for a strange land, so the religious man must willingly leave, that is, forsake a whole generation of his contemporaries even though he remains among them, but isolated, alien to them. To be an alien, to be in exile, is precisely the characteristic suffering of the religious man. (FAT-266)

1469. The Traveler Headed to London

The traveler who asked an Englishman if the road led to London and was told: Yes, it does—but he never did arrive in London, because the Englishman failed to tell him that he had to turn around, inasmuch as he was going away from London. (PF-63)

1470. The Rebellious Captain

If a prince sends a captain with a battalion of soldiers against a foreign country and that captain conquers it and then takes possession of it himself as a rebel, there is no reason to accuse him because he conquered it, but neither is there reason to celebrate because he kept it for himself—similarly, if by way of his understanding a person conquers what certainly was beautiful but yet also childish, let him not accuse understanding, but if the understanding ends with inciting mutiny, then let him not celebrate. (TDIO-26)

1471. The Government Loan Office
There is a government loan office where the poor can go. The indigent person is helped, but do the poor have a joyful conception of this loan office? Likewise, there perhaps are marriages that seek God only in adversity, alas, and seek him as a loan office; and anyone who only then seeks him always runs this danger. (TDIO-67)

1472. Man Looks, God Looks
When . . . the emperor [Napoleon] . . . led the troops and in order to inspire them said: Four hundred generations are looking down upon you—ah, just to repeat it makes one shudder—how it must have inflamed the fighters! But when we say to someone: God in heaven looks down and sees what you are doing—no one marvels, no one is moved, it is as if it meant nothing—and yet does not the eternal mean more than 4,000 years? (TDIO-114)

1473. Fear of God/City and Country
Indeed, why is it that there is more fear of God in the out-of-the-way places where there are two or three miles between each little cottage than in the noisy cities, that the sailor has more fear of God than the inhabitant of a market town. . . . In big cities both people and buildings are packed in together much too tightly. . . . There is danger that the proceeds of a person's life add up to this: he was young and still remembers many enjoyable impressions from that time, many happy days; then he was married, . . . Professor D. came and proved to be a very careful physician and thus became the family physician; also in Pastor P. he found an earnest spiritual

counselor, of whose deep religiousness and sincerity he was more convinced than of his own religiousness and therefore he became fonder of him year after year. Then he became acquainted with many congenial families, associated with them, and then he died. . . . But if this is supposed to be the ultimate when all is said and done—then I would rather not have inconvenienced either the professor or the pastor but would rather have heard the howling of the wolves and learned to know God. (SOLW-379)

1474. Seeing

According to Erasmus, Socrates was supposed to have said this to a boy. . . . When a certain wealthy man had sent his very young son to Socrates to observe his genius, and his slave said, "His father sent his son to you that you might see him, Socrates": thereupon Socrates said to the boy, "Speak lad, so that I may see you": thus signifying that the character of a man comes to light not so much in his countenance as in his manner of speaking, in which this is most certain (SOLW-730)

1475. Stopping the Train

I think that trying to restrain the age directly is as futile as for a passenger on a train to try to stop it by clutching the seat ahead of him. . . . No, the only thing to do is to get off the train and restrain oneself. (CUP-165)

1476. The Customs Clerk

Like the customs clerk who, in the belief that his business was merely to write, wrote what he himself could not read, so there are speculative thinkers who merely write, and write that which, if it is to be read with the aid of action, if I may put it that way, proves to be nonsense, unless it is perhaps intended only for fantastical beings. (CUP-191)

1477. **Praying in Truth**

If someone who lives in the midst of Christianity enters, with knowledge of the true idea of God, the house of God, the house of the true God, and prays, but prays in untruth, and if someone lives in an idolatrous land but prays with all the passion of infinity, although his eyes are resting upon the image of an idol—where, then, is there more truth? The one prays in truth to God although he is worshipping an idol; the other prays in untruth to the true God and is therefore in truth worshipping an idol. (CUP-201)

1478. **Traveling through Cities**

In the world of spirit, the different stages are not like cities on a journey, about which it is quite all right for the traveler to say directly, for example: We left Peking and came to Canton and were in Canton on the fourteenth. A traveler like that changes place, not himself; and thus it is all right for him to mention and to *recount* the change in a direct, unchanged form. But in the world of spirit to change place is to be changed oneself . . . . (CUP-281)

1479. **About Face**

During a royal review, it so happened that a major stood facing his battalion when he should have been facing the other way. An experienced army officer present, no doubt fearful that this mistake would not escape the late king's sharp scrutiny, rode over to him and whispered softly: "Major, you are facing the wrong way. You must turn around." The major was no pighead. He willingly took the advice and in a loud voice shouted, "Battalion, all together, about face!" making matters still worse. (CA-8)

1480. **Abuse**

I will suppose that there was a city where the prostitutes made a practice of abusing all the decent girls once a week, but there was one young girl who was never abused; on the contrary, she was acclaimed and praised. As young girls do, she would throw herself in tears on her mother's neck and say: Oh, Mother, why can't I be abused, too? All my friends look at me suspiciously because I am praised. But then, as mothers do, her mother would admonish patience and say, "Dear child, one does not always get what one wishes. . . ." Where the prostitutes were concerned, however, it was desirable to be abused. (CA-162)

1481. **The Bad Word**

Suppose a child comes home from playing with other children and has learned a bad word—what will happen? Well if the mother is a silly woman who chatters with other women about bringing up children, she probably will scold and slap, and in her zeal perhaps teach the child even more bad words. If, however, she is a woman who has preserved her maidenly purity, ennobled by the beautiful concern of mothering love, she would think that just because the child heard such a word once, it did not necessarily follow that it would stick with him so that he would never forget it; if he never heard it again, it would disappear without a trace as if he had never heard it—and for that very reason she would not admonish or censure him. All honor to the loving mother's quiet solicitude that daily, alertly watched over her child although externally it looked as if she were doing nothing . . . (CA-189)

1482. Reformation

It is said to have happened that a man who by his misdeeds became liable to punishment under the law returned to society a reformed man after having served his sentence. Then he went to a foreign country where he was unknown and where he became known for his upright conduct. All was forgotten; then came a fugitive who recognized the esteemed man. . . . Then despair suddenly seized the man who seemed redeemed, and it seized him just because repentance was forgotten, because this civically reformed man was still not surrendered to God in such a way that in the humility of repentance he remembered his former condition. In the temporal and sensuous and civic sense, repentance is still also something that comes and goes over the years, but in the eternal sense it is a quiet daily concern. (UDVS-18)

1483. Love and the Swallow

The most horrible collision imaginable would be a bird, for example, a swallow, in love with a girl. The swallow would be able to know the girl (as distinguished from everyone else), but the girl would not be able to tell the swallow apart from any of the 100,000 other swallows. Imagine the swallow's torment when upon its arrival in the spring it said, "Here I am" and the girl answered, "I do not know you." As a matter of fact the swallow has no individuality. We see from this that   individuality, this difference of separateness, is the presupposition for loving. . . . The greater the distinctiveness of individuality, the more pronounced the individuality, the more distinctive marks there are, and the more there is to know. (UDVS-383)

1484. **Individuality**

In this far deeper sense one sees the significance of the Hebraic expression—to know one's wife, something that was said about the difference between the genders, but the same thing is far more profoundly true about the psychical, the imprint of individuality. (UDVS-383)

1485. **The Pious Hermit**

It is told of a pious hermit, who had lived, dead to the world, for many, many years strictly observing the vow of poverty, that he had won the friendship and devotion of a rich man. Then the rich man died and bequeathed his whole fortune to the hermit, who for so long a time now had lived on the daily bread. But when someone came and told the hermit this, he answered, "There must be a mistake. How can he make me his heir when I was dead long before him!" (CD 17)

1486. **The Most Important Point**

We all know, of course, what is told about a person who had heard a story that everyone laughed at when it was told but which no one laughed at when he told it, because he, as we know, had forgotten the most important point. But imagine an apostle living in these times, an apostle who certainly knew how to tell the marvelous story properly, imagine his sadness, or the sadness of the Holy Spirit within him, when he would have to say, "There is no one who wonders; they listen to it so indifferently, as if it were the most trivial of all, as if there were no one at all to whom it applies, no one at all for whom it is of importance . . ." (CD-107)

1487. **The Author**
Imagine a person endowed, if possible, with more than extraordinary mental gifts, with a depth in pondering, a sharpness in comprehending, a clarity in expounding, a thinker the likes of whom has never been seen and never will be. He has pondered the nature of God, that God is love; he has pondered what follows from that—namely, that the world must be the best and that all things serve for good. He has recorded his ponderings in a book that is regarded as the property of the whole human race, its pride; it is translated into every language, is referred to on every scholarly occasion, is made the basis of lectures, and from this book the pastors derive their demonstrations. This thinker, protected by favorable conditions, which are indeed a necessity for scholarly research, has until now lived unacquainted with the world. Then it so happens to him that he is forced out into a decision; he must act in a difficult matter and at a decisive moment. This act is followed by a consequence such as he had least expected, a consequence that plunged him and many others into wretchedness. It is the consequence of his action—and yet he is convinced that he could not have acted in any other way than he, after the most honest deliberation, did act. Therefore the point here is not just the misfortune but that he is responsible for it, however innocent he knows he is. Now he is wounded; a doubt awakens in his soul whether this, too, can serve him for good. The direction of thought this doubt immediately takes in him, the thinker, is whether God is indeed love—in the believer doubt takes another direction, that of self-concern. Meanwhile the concern acquires more and more power over him, until finally he is at his wit's end.

In this condition he goes to a pastor who does not know him personally. He opens himself to him and seeks comfort. The clergyman who has gone along with the times and is a thinker of sorts, now wants to demonstrate to him that this, too, must be for the best and must serve him for good, since God is love, but he is soon convinced that he is not the man to enter into an intellectual bout with this stranger. After several futile attempts, the clergyman says, "Well, I know just one resource; there is a book about God's love by so and so. Read it, study it, if it cannot help you, then no one can help you." The stranger replies, "I myself am the author of that book." See, now, what the thinker had put down in that book was excellent; indeed, how would I dare question it? What the thinker had understood about God was surely also true and profound. But the thinker had not understood himself; until now he had lived under the delusion that when it had been demonstrated that God is love it followed as a matter of course that you and I believe it. As a thinker, he perhaps has taken a very dim view of faith, until—as a human being he learned to take a somewhat dimmer view of thought, especially of pure thought. The train of his thought turned around; his train of thought became different. He did not say: God is love; ergo all things serve for one's good. But he said: *When* I believe that God is love, then all things serve *me* for good. What was it that turned everything around for him—it was this "when." (CD-197)

1488. The Crowd and the Sermon

Imagine a gathering of worldly-minded, timorous people whose highest law in everything is a slavish regard for what others, what "they" will say and judge, whose sole concern is that unchristian concern that "everywhere *they* speak well" of them, whose admired goal is to be just like the others, whose sole inspiring and whose sole terrifying idea is the majority, the crowd, its approval—its disapproval. Imagine such an assembly or crowd of worshipers and devotees of the fear of people, that is, an assembly of the honored and esteemed (. . . to honor the other is, after all, to flatter oneself?)—and imagine that this assembly is supposed (yes, as it is in a comedy), is supposed to be Christian. Before this Christian assembly a sermon is delivered on these words: It is blessed to suffer mockery for a good cause! But it *is* blessed to suffer mockery for a good cause! (CD-232)

1489. The Physician's Task
The physician knows that just as there is merely imaginary sickness there is also merely imaginary health. Generally speaking, the physician, precisely because he is a physician, does not have complete confidence in what a person says about his condition. If everyone's statement about his condition, that he is healthy or sick, were completely reliable, to be a physician would be a delusion. A physician's task is not only to prescribe remedies but also, first and foremost, to identify the sickness, and consequently his first task it to ascertain whether the supposedly sick person is actually sick or whether the supposedly healthy person is perhaps actually sick. (SUD-23)

1490. Living in our House
Imagine a house with a basement, first floor, and second floor planned so that there is or is supposed to be a social distinction between the occupants according to floor. Now, if what it means to be a human being is

compared with such a house then all too regrettably the sad and ludicrous truth about the majority of people is that in their own house they prefer to live in the basement. Every human being is a psychical-physical synthesis intended to be spirit; this is the building, but he prefers to live in the basement, that is, in sensate categories. Moreover, he not only prefers to live in the basement—no, he loves it so much that he is indignant if anyone suggests that he move to the superb upper floor that stands vacant and at his disposal, for he is, after all, living in his own house. (SUD-43)

1491. **The Peasant and His New Stockings**
There is a story about a peasant who went barefooted to town with enough money to buy himself a pair of stockings and shoes and to get drunk, and in trying to find his way home in his drunken state, he fell asleep in the middle of the road. A carriage came along, and the driver shouted to him to move or he would drive over his legs. The drunken peasant woke up, looked at his legs and, not recognizing them because of the shoes and stockings, said: "Go ahead, they are not my legs." (SUD-53)

1492. **The Emperor's Son-in-Law**
If I were to imagine a poor day laborer and the mightiest emperor who ever lived, and if this mightiest emperor suddenly seized on the idea of sending for the day laborer, who had never dreamed and "in whose heart it had never arisen" that the emperor knew he existed, who then would consider himself indescribably favored just to be permitted to see the emperor once, something he would relate to his children and grandchildren as the most important event in his life—if the emperor

sent for him and told him that he wanted him for a son-in-law; what then? (SUD-84)

1493. **The Invitation**

Christianity teaches that this individual human being—and thus every single individual human being, no matter whether man, woman, servant girl, cabinet minister, merchant, barber, student, or whatever—this individual human being exists before God, this individual human being who perhaps would be proud of having spoken with the king once in his life, this human being who does not have the slightest illusion of being on intimate terms with this one or that one, this human being exists before God may speak with God any time he wants to, assured of being heard by him—in short, this person is invited to live on the most intimate terms with God! Furthermore, for this person's sake, also for this very person's sake, God comes to the world, allows himself to be born, to suffer, to die, and this suffering God—he almost implores and beseeches this person to accept the help that is offered to him! Truly, if there is anything to lose one's mind over, this is it! (SUD-85)

1494. **The King's Visit**

When a king visits a town in the provinces, he regards it as an insult if a public official fails, without sufficient cause, to pay his respects to him; but I wonder what he would think if someone were to ignore completely the fact that the king was in town and played the private citizen who says: "The devil take His Majesty and the Royal Law." This is the way a man talks pretentiously about what he basically ignores—and thus pretentiously ignores God. (SUD-130)

1495. **The Rich Man and his Team of Horses**
Once upon a time there was a rich man. At an exorbitant price he had purchased abroad a team of entirely flawless, splendid horses, which he had wanted for his own pleasure and the pleasure of driving them himself. About a year or two passed by. If anyone who had known these horses earlier now saw him driving them, he would not be able to recognize them; their eyes had become dull and drowsy; their gait lacked style and precision; they had no staying power, no endurance; he could drive them scarcely four miles without having to stop on the way, and sometimes they came to a standstill just when he was driving his best; moreover, they had acquired all sort of quirks and bad habits, and although they of course had plenty of feed they grew thinner day by day. Then he called in the royal coachman. He drove them for a month. In the whole countryside there was not a team of horses that carried their heads so proudly, whose eyes were so fiery, whose gait was so beautiful; there was no team of horses that could hold out running as they did, even thirty miles in a stretch without stopping. How did this happen? It is easy to see: the owner, who without being a coachman meddled with being a coachman, drove the horses according to the horses' understanding of what it is to drive; the royal coachman drove them according to the coachman's understanding of what it is to drive. (FSE-85)

1496. **Quantity**
There is an amusing story about a saloonkeeper. . . . He is said to have sold his bottled beer for a cent under the purchase price, and when someone said to him: "How does that pay? Indeed, you are losing money," he answered, "No, my friend, it is the quantity that does it"—

the quantity, which indeed also in our day is omnipotent. When one has laughed at this story, one does well to heed the moral, which warns against the power that numbers exercise over the imagination. (M-36)

1497. **The Source of the Spring**
If an Arab in the desert were suddenly to discover a spring in his tent, and so would always be able to have water in abundance, how fortunate he would consider himself—so too, when a man who *qua* physical being is always turned towards the outside, thinking that his happiness lies outside him finally turns inward and discovers that the source is within him; not to mention his discovering that the source is his relation to God. *Journals* (KA-108)

1498. **The Tame Geese**
Suppose it was so that the geese could talk—then they had so arranged it that they also could have their religious worship, their divine service. Every Sunday they came together, and one of the ganders preached. The essential content of the sermon was: what a lofty destiny the geese had, what a high goal the Creator (and every time this word was mentioned the geese curtsied and the ganders bowed the head) had set before the geese; by the aid of wings they could fly away to distant regions, blessed climes, where properly they were at home, for here they were only strangers. So it was every Sunday. And as soon as the assembly broke up each waddled home to his own affairs. And then the next Sunday again to divine worship and then again home—and that was the end of it, they throve and were well-liking, became plump and delicate—and then were eaten on Martinmas Eve—and that was the end of it. That

was the end of it. For though the discourse sounded so lofty on Sunday, the geese on Monday were ready to recount to one another what befell a goose that had wanted to make serious use of the wings the Creator had given him, designed for the high goal that was proposed to him—what befell him, what a terrible death he encountered. This the geese could talk about knowingly among themselves. But, naturally, to speak about it on Sundays was unseemly; for, said they, it would then become evident that our divine worship is really only making a fool of God and of ourselves. Among the geese there were, however, some individuals which seemed suffering and grew thin. About them it was currently said among the geese: There you see what it leads to when flying is taken seriously. For because their hearts are occupied with the thought of wanting to fly, therefore they become thin, do not thrive, do not have the grace of God as we have who therefore become plump and delicate. And so the next Sunday they went again to divine worship, and the old gander preached about the high goal the Creator (here again the geese curtsied and the ganders bowed the head) had set before the geese, whereto the wings were designed. So with the divine worship of Christendom. Man also has wings, he has imagination . . . *Journals* (KA-433)

1499. **Haste**

It is said of Till Eulenspiegel that he was sent to town by his mistress to fetch four shillings' worth of vinegar. He was away for nearly three years. Toward the end of the third year, he came charging in at the door, broke the flask to pieces, spilled the vinegar, and cried: "The devil created haste." (EPW-217)

1500. A King Who Visits Every Day

If a king were to visit a humble family—yes, the family would feel honored, proud, almost overwhelmed by their good fortune. But if his majesty were to keep on visiting the same family every day, how long would it be before the king would almost have to make an effort to find a little meaning in his visiting the family, who out of habit went on saying without change: We thank you for the great honor. (CD-315)

1501. Accustomed to Unfaithfulness

There is a man whose wife is unfaithful to him, but he does not know it. Then one of his friends enlightens him about it—a dubious act of friendship, many will perhaps say. The man replies: It is with intense interest that I have listened to you speak. . . . But that I should therefore, now that I know it is so, divorce her—no, that I cannot decide to do. After all, I am accustomed to this domestic routine; I cannot do without it. Moreover she has money; I cannot do without that either. On the other hand . . . it is extremely interesting. . . . Similarly, there is also something frightful in this: to be aware in the form of interesting information that one's worship is blasphemy and then to continue in it because, after all, one is accustomed to it. (M-259)

1502. Going to the Deer Park

Let us assume that it is God's will that we human beings must not go to Deer Park. Naturally "humankind" would not accept this. What would happen then? What would happen is that "the pastors" would make out that when, for example, one blessed the four-seated Holstein carriage and made the sign of the cross over the horses, then going to Deer Park would become well-pleasing to God. (M-348)

1503. **The Banknote**

Let me illustrate. In a town there lives a stranger; he possesses only one banknote, but one that is of a very large denomination. But no one in the town recognizes the banknote; to them it = 0, and of course no one will give him anything for the paper note. Then a man comes alone, a stranger, for example, who recognizes the banknote very well and says to him one day, "I am your friend, and, as befits a friend, I will help you out of your predicament, I offer you"—and then he offers him half its value. See, this is sophisticated! It is calculated to look like friendship and devotedness, which must be admired and praised by the inhabitants of that town and at the same time to cheat out of fifty percent. . . . As in money matters, so in matter of the spirit. (M-351)

1504. **The Defective Throne**

There are many excellent stories in . . . A Thousand and One Nights—for example. . . . About the poor couple who prayed to God for a little help, and he let a ruby fall down. They rejoiced greatly. But that night the wife dreamed that she was in paradise and saw the countless pulpits and thrones. When she asked for whom they were, she was told that they were for the prophets, for the righteous and the pious. She asked if there was one for her husband. It was shown to her—but she noticed a chink on one side, and it was explained to her that this chink signified the ruby that had fallen down to them. Then she became despondent, implored her husband to pray God to take the ruby back. "It is better to endure poverty these few days than to have to sit among glorious ones on a throne that has a defect." (M-394)

1505. **The Swimming Instructor**
. . . When the swimming instructor himself leaps into the deep water and then says to the beginner that he will help him, that there is nothing to be afraid of—the teacher expects one thing—that the beginner will leap out into the deep water. If the beginner gets the notion of walking out in the shallows and playing at swimming—that makes a fool of the swimming instructor, who is ready and waiting out in the deep water. (M-468)

1506. **It will be a Frightful Night**
Imagine a very large ship, even larger than the great ships we have today. Let it have room for one thousand passengers and, of course, everything planned as conveniently and comfortably and luxuriously etc. on the largest scale possible. It is evening. In the lounge there is gaiety, everything is beautifully illuminated, everything glitters, the orchestra is playing; in short, all is merriment, frivolity, enjoyment—and the racket and noise from the happy, hilarious fun rings out into the night. Up on the deck stands the captain, and with him the second in command. The latter takes the telescope from his eye and hands it to the captain. He replies: "I do not need it; I see it all right, the little white speck on the horizon—it will be a frightful night." Thereupon, with the noble, resolute calmness of the experienced seaman, he issues his orders: "The crew will remain on duty tonight; I myself will take command." He goes into his cabin. He has not taken an especially large library along, but he has a Bible. He opens it and,

curiously enough, he opens it up to the passage: In this night your soul will be required of you. Curious! After his prayers he dresses for night duty, and now he is the full-fledged able-bodied seaman. But the frivolity goes on in the lounge. There is song and music and conversation and noise, the clatter of plates and dishes; the champagne bottles pop, toasts are drunk to the captain, etc. etc.—"It will be a frightful night"—and perhaps this night your soul will be required of you. Is this not frightful? And yet I know something still more frightful. Everything is the same, only the captain is different. The lounge is full of gaiety, and the gayest of them all is the captain. The white speck on the horizon is there; it will be a frightful night. But no one sees the white speck or suspects what it means. But no (this would not be the most frightful)—no, there is one person who sees it and knows what it means—but he is a passenger. He has, after all, no commission on the ship; he cannot do anything. But in order to do the one single thing he can do, he asks the captain to come up on deck, only for a moment. It takes a while, but finally he comes—but does not wish to hear anything and, passing it off as a joke, hurries down to the noisy, hilarious company in the lounge, where the toasts are being drunk to the captain with the usual enthusiasm, for which he thanks affably. In his anxiety the poor passenger decides to dare once again to inconvenience the captain, but this time he is even impolite to him. But the white speck is still there on the horizon—"It will be a frightful night." (M-511)

At any rate, I prize coffee. (R-170)

Key to Sources— Books in Alphabetical Order

<table>
<tr><td>BOA</td><td>The Book on Adler
Edited and Translated By Howard V. Hong and Edna H. Hong
Princeton University Press, Princeton, New Jersey, 1998</td></tr>
<tr><td>CA</td><td>The Corsair Affair
Søren Kierkegaard Edited and Translated by Howard V. Hong and Edna H. Hong
Princeton University Press, Princeton, New Jersey, 1982</td></tr>
<tr><td>CD</td><td>Christian Discourses
The Crisis and a Crisis in the Life of an Actress
Edited and Translated by Howard V. Hong and Edna H. Hong
Princeton University Press, Princeton, New Jersey, 1997</td></tr>
</table>

COA	*The Concept of Anxiety* *A Simple Psychologically Orienting Deliberation on the Dogmatic Issue of Hereditary Sin* Edited and Translated by Reidar Thomte in Collaboration with Albert B. Anderson Princeton University Press, Princeton, New Jersey, 1980
COI	*The Concept of Irony* *with Continual Reference to Socrates* Translated and Edited by Howard V. and Edna H. Hong Princeton University Press, Princeton, New Jersey, 1992
CUP	*Concluding Unscientific Postscript to Philosophical Fragments* Edited and Translated by Howard V. Hong and Edna H. Hong Princeton university Press, Princeton, New Jersey, 1992
D	*The Diary of Søren Kierkegaard* Ed. By Peter P. Rohde Philosophical Library, Carol Publishing Group, New York, 1993
E/O I	*Either / Or PART I* Edited and Translated by Howard V. Hong and Edna H. Hong Princeton University Press, Princeton, New Jersey, 1987
E/O II	*Either / Or PART II* Edited and Translated by Howard V. Hong and Edna H. Hong Princeton University Press, Princeton, New Jersey, 1987

EPW	*Early Polemical Writings* Edited and Translated by Julia Watkin Princeton University Press, Princeton, New Jersey, 1990
EUD	*Eighteen Upbuilding Discourses* Edited and Translated by Howard V. Hong and Edna H. Hong Princeton University Press, Princeton, New Jersey, 1990
FAT/R	*Fear and Trembling/Repetition* Edited and Translated by Howard V. Hong and Edna H. Hong Princeton University Press, Princeton, New Jersey, 1983
FSE/JFY	*For Self-Examination/Judge for Yourself* Translated by Howard V. Hong and Edna H. Hong Princeton University Press, Princeton, New Jersey, 1990
KA	*A Kierkegaard Anthology* Edited By Robert Bretall Princeton University Press, Princeton, New Jersey, 1946
M	*The Moment and Late Writings* Edited and Translated by Howard V. Hong and Edna H. Hong Princeton University Press, Princeton, New Jersey, 1998
P	*Prefaces/Writing Sampler* Nicolaus Notabene Edited and Translated by Todd W. Nichol Princeton U. Press, Princeton, New Jersey, 1997

PF	*Philosophical Fragments* by Johannes Climacus Edited and Translated by Howard V. Hong and Edna H. Hong Princeton University Press, Princeton, New Jersey, 1985
PIC	*Practice in Christianity* Translated and Edited by Howard V. Hong and Edna H. Hong Princeton Paperback, Princeton university Press, 1991
POV	*The Point of View* Edited and Translated by Howard V. Hong and Edna H. Hong Princeton University Press, Princeton, New Jersey, 1998
SOLW	*Stages on Life's Way* Edited and Translated by Howard V. Hong and Edna H. Hong Princeton University Press, Princeton, New Jersey, 1988
SUD	*The Sickness unto Death* A Christian Psychological Exposition for Upbuilding and Awakening Translated and Edited by Howard Hong and Edna Hong Princeton University Press, 1983
TA	*Two Ages The Age of Revolution and the Present Age* Edited and Translated by Howard V. Hong and Edna H. Hong Princeton University Press, Princeton, New Jersey, 1978

TDIO   *Three Discourses on Imagined Occasions*
                 Edited and Translated by Howard V. And
                 Edna H. Hong
                 Princeton University Press, Princeton, New
                 Jersey, 1993
UDVS   *Upbulding Discourses in Various Spirits*
                 Edited and Translated by Howard V. Hong
                 and Edna H. Hong
                 Princeton University Press, Princeton, New
                 Jersey, 1993
WA   *Without Authority*
                 Edited and Translated by Howard V. Hong
                 and Edna H. Hong
                 Princeton University Press, Princeton, New
                 Jersey, 1997
WOL   *Works of Love*
                 Edited and Translated by Howard V. Hong
                 and Edna H. Hong
                 Princeton University Press, Princeton, New
                 Jersey, 1995

Books in Order of Publication

1. EPW	Early Polemical Writings (1838)
2. COI	The Concept of Irony (1841)
3. E/O I	Either/Or Part I (1843)
4. E/O II	Either/Or Part II (1843)
5. EUD	Eighteen Upbuilding Discourses (1843–44)
6. FAT/R	Fear and Trembling / Repetition (1843)
7. PF	Philosophical Fragments (1844)
8. COA	The Concept of Anxiety (1844)
9. P	Prefaces / Writing Sampler (1844)
10. TDIO	Three Discourses on Imagined Occasions (1844)
11. SOLW	Stages on Life's Way (1845)
12. CUP	Concluding Unscientific Postscript (1845)
13. CA	The Corsair Affair (1845)
14. TA	Two Ages (1846)
15. UDVS	Upbulding Discourses in Various Spirits (1847)
16. WOL	Works of Love (1847)

17. CD	Christian Discourses/Crisis in the Life of an Actress (1848)
18. WA	Without Authority (1849–50)
19 SUD	The Sickness unto Death (1849)
20 PIC	Practice in Christianity (1850)
21 FSE/JFY	For Self-Examination/Judge for Yourself (1851)
22 POV	The Point of View (1859—written earlier)
23 M	The Moment and Late Writings (1854–55)
24 BOA	The Book on Adler (1872)

Summary and Evaluation of Books

E*arly Polemical Writings* (1838)—beginning in 1834 during student days—are witty and urbane, but hardly Christian. They contain a few of his later themes and the beginning of some of his Christian insights. Notable among them is his negative review of a novel by his contemporary, Hans Christian Andersen, whom he considered not to have "a life view." He himself did not consider these writings as part of his oeuvre. The most significant event of these years from the standpoint of K's Christianity is his conversion—an experience dated in his *Journal* as occurring on May 19, 1838, at half-past ten in the morning. It was described in his diary as one of "indescribable joy" (an experience very reminiscent of that of Paschal). It was followed immediately by reconciliation with his family.

The Concept of Irony with Continual Reference to Socrates (1841) is Kierkegaard's Master's Thesis (his degree entitled him to be referred to as "Magister"). He had entered the University of Copenhagen in 1830 and pursued his studies desultorily until 1841, when he wrote and defended his thesis. During this period he met (she was 15 and he was 24), fell in love with, and finally rejected Regine Olsen in a famous failed romance. This book shows K's genius in his ability to create metaphor and in his insight into the classical Greek mind—insight that easily equals that of Nietzsche. It displays concepts that will transition into his later Christian themes. This is a very long book to read just to glean a few of K's incipient Christian insights.

Either/Or Part I (1843) is Kierkegaard's most successful work from the standpoint of sales, and he considered it to be the beginning of his oeuvre as an author. From this point on to the midpoint of his career as an author, he produced signed Christian works along with unsigned (pseudonymous) secular works. He considered pseudonymity to be a mark of distancing ("a bill of divorcement") from personal attachment to what was said. For his signed works, however, he took full and direct responsibility. Little of *Either/Or Part I* is of specifically Christian interest, but the esthetic analysis of (operatic) music and literature is brilliant. One section, *The Seducer's Diary*, is a tour-de-force famous for its pioneering insights into the psychology of the human mind and the psychology (existential inwardness) of seduction. It was no doubt written from the standpoint of his romance with Regine Olsen.

Either/Or Part II (1843) contains much of interest to the Christian, including an emphasis on ethics and passages of literary beauty. This second of the two volumes discloses the subject indicated in the title. Kierkegaard was a lifelong opponent of the teaching of Hegel (both /and, synthesis, etc.), and he believed that life's most important choices had the form of *Either/Or*. Even so neither volume of *Either/Or* is, in my opinion, the right place to start in getting to know Kierkegaard as a Christian author; although it is the place where most students are encouraged to start—perhaps with a more secular viewpoint in mind.

Eighteen Upbuilding Discourses (1843–44) contains a compilation of Christian writings that Kierkegaard produced in parallel with his pseudonymous works. These are signed works. They argue directly to the purpose of making persons aware of the essentially Christian. These were not well received in contemporary Danish society probably because (expressing Kierkegaard's viewpoint) secular society wishes to remain undisturbed in its pleasures even if it means remaining deceived.

Fear and Trembling & Repetition (1843) are published together in one volume. *Fear and Trembling* is a meditation on God's demand that Abraham sacrifice Isaac. In this book Kierkegaard asserts that Abraham "had faith by virtue of the absurd." This saying is as perplexing as Tertullian's [attributed] comment, "I believe because it is absurd." It has been latched on to by those who would criticize Kierkegaard for lack of objectivity in his analysis of faith. Little of Kierkegaard's subsequent writing makes this phrase definitive for his total output, but its onus has stuck. The book's analysis of Abraham's faith is quite helpful, and it is full of those peculiar insights typical of genius. *Repetition* is a kind of psychological testing of the possibility (and also the impossibility) of repeating an experience. One repeats by going on, but it is never the identical experience. *Repetition* is psychologically insightful, but has little to offer one looking for Christian insights.

Philosophical Fragments (1844) contains musings on philosophical issues such as the possibility of learning anything new, even if God is the teacher, and philosophical issues surrounding doubt. Does philosophy begin with doubt or wonder? Answer: It begins with wonder. Here is Kierkegaard's brilliant solution to the barrier of "Lessing's Ditch" (Accidental truths of history can never become the proof of necessary truths of reason.) The historical is made universal by incarnation. All in all there is little else to interest the Christian reader here.

The Concept of Anxiety (1844) is a meditation on original and pervasive (persistent) sin. It ascribes sin to our freedom of choice. Free choice by its very nature exposes us to doubt, to the "dizziness of freedom," to possibility, and therefore to anxiety. (This idea is cited repeatedly as pre-Freudian.) Kierkegaard's analysis is totally Christian. Freedom is the basis for "The Fall," and this "Fall" is taken seriously as sin before God. Kierkegaard's persistent criticism of classical Greek thinking was that it lacked the concept of the will. This book provides fresh and helpful insights into our sin nature.

Prefaces & Writing Sampler (1844) are both witty; the latter is also silly. The various "Prefaces" are composed as if he were writing prefaces to books, but not the books themselves. They have little of Christian interest.

Three Discourses on Imagined Occasions (1844) is the last of his signed works that parallel his series of pseudonymous works during the "first half" of his authorship. These are "imagined" so that they would not offend. The first deals with confession—stillness and wonder in seeking God; the second contains Christian observations on marriage; and the third is a meditation on death. First Rate. Kierkegaard's viewpoints are original, unique and helpful.

Stages on Life's Way (1845) is intended to improve *Either/Or* by revisiting its issues from a more Christian standpoint. It is a reworking of Plato's Symposium. There are three existence-spheres (stages) for mankind: the esthetic, the ethical, and the religious. Worthwhile Christian reading.

Concluding Unscientific Postscript to Philosophical Fragments (1845) is the "midpoint" of Kierkegaard's work as an author. "Unscientific" does not mean illogical. It means unsystematic, individual, existential; and therefore not subject to averaging or "scientific' generalization. "Lessing's Ditch" (Accidental truths of history can never become the proof of necessary truths of reason) is "leaped" with panache, and the ditch itself made into an accidental truth. This is my favorite among K's pseudonymous works. Read it.

The Corsair Affair (1845) contains the articles written by Kierkegaard during his famous feud with the newspapers and literary opinion-makers of Copenhagen. The Corsair was the name of the main newspaper involved. The personal attacks on Kierkegaard were vicious and destructive. They did one positive thing, however. They made him renew his authorship. The few Christian opinions expressed here are heartfelt and penetrating. The Christian opinions that follow in the "second half" of his authorship, occurring in the ensuing few years of his life, are his very best.

Two Ages (1846) is a lengthy book review that became more important and more enduring than the book itself. There are many astute observations on the age that are pertinent to our own along with a few Christian insights. Human nature remains the same.

Upbuilding Discourses in Various Spirits (1847) contains two of Kierkegaard's most famous essays: *Purity of Heart Is to Will One Thing*. This portion alone makes this volume worth reading. The rest of the discourses are marvelous. The third section has also been separately published as *The Gospel of Sufferings*. It will be your privilege to see Christianity through the eyes of a believing genius.

Works of Love (1847) is Kierkegaard's description of the highest the individual can achieve—personal love (self-yielding) toward God and personal love (self-giving) in imitation of Christ. Read it. There is nothing like it—not in Kierkegaard, not anywhere else.

Christian Discourses & The Crisis and a Crisis in the Life of an Actress (1848) is an odd combination in one volume of two different kinds of works. The latter of the two works displays Kierkegaard's artistically perceptive critical faculties. The former matches any and all of the other Christian discourses. It includes seven meditations on *Communion, Discourses at the Communion on Fridays,* that provide thoughtful insight into that sacrament's meaning, and what it means to know and be known to God.

Without Authority (1849–50) is the disclaimer Kierkegaard applied to many sermons or religious teachings that he proffered to the public. He believed that he did not have the authority of an ordained clergyman. Here is a collection of his sermons (*Discourses*) and religious essays that he would claim to be "without authority." From such an author they have lots of authority. Highly recommended.

The Sickness unto Death (1849) is a meditation on sin. Sin is sinful because it is before God. If we despair, we sin. If we are inexcusably weak or defiant, we sin. If we sin and are unforgiven, we truly have the sickness unto death which is ultimate despair (hopelessness). Here is another book that the psychoanalysts like to quote. Fair enough, but it is a thoroughly Christian treatise.

Practice in Christianity (1850) is Kierkegaard's definitive, public attack on formal Christianity and on personally uncommitted Christians. A scathing criticism of officialdom that is as modern and pertinent today as then. Mainline Christianity, take heed!

For Self-Examination & Judge for Yourself (1851) continue the intellectual narrative of K's struggle with the Danish Church. These are more inward and thoughtful criticisms of officialdom than *Practice in Christianity.* The first of the two challenges the Christian to measure his life by 1) the Word of God; 2) the Imitation of Christ;

and 3) Life in the Spirit. The second bids us judge our Christian lives by looking soberly at ourselves and letting Christ be our prototype. This book is a good (perhaps the best) beginning to reading Kierkegaard.

The Point of View (1859, but written earlier) is a compilation of two major and several minor publications in which Kierkegaard examines and explains his own work as an author. It is clear that he views himself as a Christian author trying to re-introduce Christianity into Christendom, a battle of "the individual" against the crowd.

The Moment & Late Writings (1854–55) is another compilation—a collection of his writings relating the public aspect of the controversy between Kierkegaard and the official church. At the death of Bishop Mynster (1854), whom Kierkegaard opposed but revered, he lays aside subtlety, and issues withering and sarcastic criticisms of the church and its leaders. He was particularly offended by Bishop Hans Lassen Martensen, his former professor and successor to Mynster, who eulogized Mynster as a "witness to the truth." This book shows Kierkegaard in high dudgeon, even trying to provoke a fight. The perspective is monomaniacal and bitterly sarcastic—but perhaps with reason.

The Book on Adler (1872) is the last published book by Kierkegaard. It was written nearly at the midpoint of his authorship, but it was not published until well after his death. Here Kierkegaard criticizes Hegelianism and purely subjective opinions. A Danish clergyman, Adolph P. Adler, claimed to have received a special revelation from God. It is clear especially from this book (but others as well) that Kierkegaard believed in objective truth, especially the definitive and normative revelation of God in Scripture. Kierkegaard's so-called subjective "leap of faith" was subjective only in the sense that the individual must do it on his own initiative.

The final volumes listed are miscellaneous in subject. *The Diary of Søren Kierkegaard* is a publication of personal thoughts, not published, that in many places repeat information in the public writings from a different viewpoint. The *Kierkegaard Anthology* is a sampling of his writings selected to introduce the author and his thoughts.

If I wished to begin to read Kierkegaard for myself from a Christian viewpoint I would begin with the book containing *For Self-Examination* and *Judge for Yourself*. Another entry into Kierkegaard's Christian thought would be any book with *Discourses* in the title. None of these works is too very long. The first suggestion is probably the best.

Have happy and blessed reading!

Index

Abandoned	12, 95, 768	Adultery	334
Abraham	288, 885, 899, 900, 1468	Adversity	279, 280, 459, 1002, 1471
Absolute (ly)	3, 133, 187, 291, 495, 531, 577, 598, 601, 603, 604, 606, 734, 735, 901 911, 915, 927, 974, 1039, 1068	Age (chronological)	387, 705, 878, 1019, 1042, 1347
Abstraction	108, 191, 192, 1071, 1163, 1207	Age (the)	44, 190, 230, 335, 340, 429, 484, 585, 782, 829, 1119, 1142, 1152, 1158, 1161, 1162, 1210, 1236, 1332
Absurd (the)	288, 1280	Agrippa (King)	675
Acoustic	1381	Alcohol	1218
Actor, Actress	619, 1347, 1445	Alien, Alienated	321, 352, 1468
Actuality	103, 819, 955, 968, 1099, 1164, 1248, 1422	Alone	52, 202, 536, 670, 722, 746, 795, 870, 1100, 1116, 1216
Adage	388, 1436	Altar	79, 420, 1302
Adler	1103, 1262	Amager	817
Admiration	41, 225, 623, 757, 758, 760-762, 1098, 1144, 1192, 1194, 1488, 1503	Ambiguity	135, 1059

Index

Ancestors   1466
Angel   276, 564
Animal,
   Animalistic   109, 775, 925, 1155, 1253, 1391
Anxiety   251, 492, 636, 637, 1093, 1283, 1285, 1506
Ape   1304
Apostle   14, 95, 96, 461, 684, 705, 1103, 1123, 1157, 1169, 1191, 1304, 1399, 1486
Approxi-
   mation   580, 1447
Arab   1497
Archimedean
   point   27
Aristocratic   147, 1423
Aristotle   1289
Asceticism   335
Atheist   330, 362
Attorney   1275
Authentic   366, 485, 1006
Authority   170, 266, 425, 429, 455, 461, 1119, 1124, 1125
Autopsy   243
Autumn   1405, 1418
Average   125, 1401, 1413
Baker   1200
Banal   94, 340, 384
Bank, Bank-
   note   389, 1446, 1503
Bankruptcy   1264
Barber   1416, 1493
Barrels   159, 1212
Bass Part   31

Battle   707, 1151, 1408
Battlefield   1408
Beatitude   1147
Beautiful   159, 785, 827, 868, 869, 946, 949, 964, 986, 992, 1014, 1021, 1101, 1284, 1415, 1470, 1481, 1495
Behrend
   (minister)   1420
Betray   95, 228, 646, 658, 987
Bible   1021, 1506
Bird(s)   31, 587, 840-842, 860, 1483
Blasphemy   71, 527, 754, 1501
Blessed   66, 151, 301, 427, 510, 610, 642, 692, 891, 931, 987, 1027, 1488, 1498
Blessing   53, 77, 98, 153, 459, 842
Blindness   156, 586
Book of
   formulas   24
Bread   610, 840-842, 847, 1087, 1485
Bully   1341
Business   700, 1438, 1476
Buy, Buyer   355, 1171, 1271, 1491
Cannon   1460
Canton
   (China)   1478
Capital
   Crimes   154, 155
Captive   240, 909

Index

Category (ies) 170, 231, 234,
336, 338, 398,
496, 674. 1098,
1292, 1447, 1490
Cemetery 448
Certainty 243, 276, 322,
511, 974, 1298
Chitchat 1400
Changeless
(One) 26, 64, 66, 1376
Choice 187, 591, 592,
617, 618, 679,
683, 694, 695
Choose 187, 188, 591,
693, 746, 747,
881, 1030, 1398
Chosen 591, 592, 649,
679, 1232
Church 159, 327, 331,
336, 341, 364,
385, 417, 865,
1099, 1406, 1423
Cities 212, 249, 1173,
1200, 1473, 1478,
1480
Coffee 354, 1507
Comedy,
Comic 192, 566, 789, 872,
940, 1415, 1488
Comfort 60, 245, 309, 462,
550, 581, 700,
734, 1050, 1431,
1487
Committee 369, 1069, 1385
Communal 1163
Communion 931
Communion
(table) 42, 222, 223, 312,
313
Communism 324

Comparison 436, 538, 809,
839, 978, 1248
Compel 114, 179, 529,
805, 994
Conceal 385, 458, 781,
1220, 1250
Conception 5, 8, 27, 36, 46,
114, 246, 280,
642, 723, 1003,
1153, 1258, 1471
Concretion 108, 216, 1163
Confession 48, 70, 118, 202,
305, 314, 318,
348, 540, 546,
547, 699, 828,
1081
Congregation 222, 364, 1087,
1102
Conquer 99, 333, 655, 724,
873, 1002, 1354,
1439, 1464, 1466,
1470
Conscience 199, 219, 770,
1015, 1134, 1157
Consolation 742
Constipation 1391
Contem-
porary 260, 515, 634,
703, 735, 761,
829, 911, 1063,
1098, 1164, 1194,
1214, 1332, 1468
Contract 556
Contradiction 133, 272, 542,
888, 910, 972,
1070, 1127
Convenient 342, 924, 1388,
1473, 1506
Conversation 214, 772, 1239,
1240, 1506

Copenhagen 158, 1264

Corrupt (ion) 156, 307, 422
433, 442, 449,
561, 1150, 1167,
1170, 1253, 1373

Corsair 166, 1202

Country 159, 171, 357,
361, 1174, 1189,
1446, 1470, 1473

Cowardliness 569, 575-577,

Cowardly 507, 708, 999,
1205, 1341

Crave 259, 281, 352,
453, 639, 697,
870, 1324

Craven 422

Create 5, 32, 53, 113,
206, 393, 554,
559, 779, 808,
910, 1032, 1139,
1163, 1164, 1203,
1499

Creation 276, 427, 910

Creed 714

Crossroads 683

Crowd 145, 159, 194,
195, 199, 200,
262, 263, 266,
539, 541, 629,
806, 1061, 1209,
1236, 1291, 1417,
1488

Crown 71, 967

Crown of
thorns 71

Crucify (ied) 75, 94, 95, 384,
658

Culture 317, 325, 334,
335, 393, 571,

719, 1119, 1154,
1236

Cup (the) 1056, 1465

Custom,
accustomed 160, 311, 354,
490, 1210, 1460,
1461, 1501

Curse,
Cursing 336, 1210

Danger,
Dangerous 9, 72, 228, 230,
318, 343, 356,
365, 381, 383,
394, 421, 436,
461, 616, 659,
690, 707, 708,
738, 761, 773,
794, 796, 811,
1074, 1087, 1088,
1098, 1160, 1186,
1222, 1302, 1319,
1331, 1429, 1471,
1473,

Dead 448, 503, 519,
525, 1299, 1485

Death 94, 179, 276, 365,
384, 643, 657,
659, 660, 738,
771, 795, 815,
917, 918, 1226,
1298, 1317, 1424

Debauchery 141, 1294

Debt, Debtor 855, 976, 978,
1337

Deceive 247, 259, 429,
453, 458, 493,
769, 980, 1186,
1220-1223, 1227,
1237, 1271, 1377,
1378

Deception
    (self)   259, 453, 970,
           1224, 1229
Decide   119, 130, 607,
           645, 715, 1058,
           1501
Decision   148, 274, 512,
           674, 675, 677,
           710, 908, 1029,
           1487
Decisive   15, 244, 342, 493,
           597, 625, 649,
           652-654, 661,
           703, 881, 1025,
           1050, 1131, 1251,
           1437
Defiance   379, 422, 430,
           440, 495, 1374
Deliver (er)   240, 635
Delphi   60
Delusion   71, 358, 619, 733,
           761, 1103, 1272,
           1350, 1487, 1489
Demand(s)   30, 130, 209, 419,
           742, 766, 816, 891,
           1073, 1091, 1200,
           1210, 1243, 1247,
           1438
Demonic   573
Demonstrate   33, 39, 244, 270,
           275, 389, 424,
           652, 692, 763,
           831, 1061, 1135,
           1308, 1487
Demoralize   1217
Denmark   157, 167, 182,
           316, 1421
Dependence   114, 981, 1328
Depravity   1014, 1426
De profundis   31

Descartes   1386
Desire   40, 95, 116, 117,
           122, 127, 139,
           251, 281, 590,
           604, 806, 933,
           1223, 1247, 1248,
           1480
Devil   128, 454, 495,
           1171, 1290, 1442,
           1494, 1499
Diabolical   709
Diagnosis   372,
Dialectic,
    Dialectical   114, 135, 190,
           500, 660, 792,
           793, 1103, 1161
Die   14, 29, 104, 211,
           507, 518, 620,
           636, 761, 922,
           928, 1019, 1089,
           1317, 1473, 1485,
           1493
Die to
    (the world)   25, 253, 515, 524,
           525, 527
Disagreement   64, 267, 395
Disclose   396, 458, 617,
           693, 1285
Discourse   109, 436, 1043,
           1459
Dishonor   707
Disobedience   427-429, 615
Disorder   738
Distance   164, 776, 798,
           1176, 1344, 1347
Distance
    (from God)   7, 17, 23
Distinction   134, 152, 159,
           366, 485, 539,

Index

566, 628, 710, 864, 972, 1292, 1436, 1483, 1490

Divine
    worship   42, 43, 364, 1010, 1498

Doctrine   342, 905, 1035, 1089, 1120

Don Juan   940

Double-
  mindedness   136-138, 405, 407-409

Drama   1143

Drink   390, 507, 636, 1144, 1218, 1418, 1464, 1465

Dropsy   331

Drunk   1491, 1506

Duty   248, 336, 425, 712, 879, 880, 882, 955, 972, 1001, 1506

Dwell   468, 492, 550, 864, 977

Dying   521, 554, 632, 738, 1153

Dying
(to the world)   335, 342

Earnest,
  Earnestness   284, 334, 347, 370, 393, 486, 504, 506, 509, 711, 803, 820, 878, 1030, 1117, 1119, 1172, 1473

Earth   17, 23, 84, 92, 229, 353, 386, 523, 565, 657, 733, 747, 749, 847, 1091, 1146, 1405

Earthly   276, 436, 525, 631, 633, 639, 640, 655, 833, 844, 856, 860, 936, 1147, 1169

Earthquake   628, 706

Eclipse   523

Educate   335, 475-477, 1103

Eloquence   1033, 1255, 1295

Eminent   24, 190, 578, 727, 729

Emotion   1127, 1257, 1258, 1445

Emperor   727, 1098, 1472, 1492

England,
  English   502, 1469

Enjoyment   343, 454, 464, 866, 951, 1137, 1463, 1506

En Masse   213

Entertain-
    ment   1092, 1206

Environment   834

Envy, Envious   769, 1317, 1321, 1322

Equality   190, 193, 216, 235, 265, 268, 322, 324, 392, 508-510, 721, 798, 956-958, 1034, 1060, 1063, 1195, 1327, 1331, 1383

Erasmus   1474

Europe   1196, 1421

Evasion   218, 251, 707

Evil   119, 178, 217, 332, 574, 623,

Examine
  (ation) 85, 1399
Excuse 251, 481
External,
  Externality 90, 101, 109, 158, 194, 439, 465, 584, 729, 738, 802, 875, 1155, 1157, 1481
Extraordinary 28, 84, 103, 173, 330, 376, 377, 710, 732, 1097, 1098, 1487
Fall (the) 59, 123, 379, 434
False 28, 251, 332, 432, 698, 734, 1045, 1207, 1293
Fat 331
Fate 36, 398, 494
Father 11, 27, 29, 228, 387, 932, 1174, 1219, 1230, 1353, 1468, 1474
Feathers 1436
Finite 469, 532, 600, 604, 888, 898, 1037, 1059, 1152, 1387, 1411, 1452
Fire 1389, 1462
Flesh 67, 115, 128, 723, 948, 1363
Follower 86, 650, 654, 748, 758, 761, 1076
Fool 200, 347, 1204, 1276, 1407, 1411, 1498, 1505
635, 658, 698, 781, 855, 1160, 1170, 1208, 1209, 1255, 1409
Foolishness 317, 377, 616, 723, 1184, 1313, 1366, 1437, 1444
Forbidden 55, 122, 1212
Forget 59, 79, 221, 246, 249, 295, 369, 431, 432, 436, 513, 559, 563, 616, 627, 838, 844, 875, 876, 988, 1045, 1362, 1364, 1433, 1481
Forgive (ness) 76, 83, 167, 295, 302, 445, 535, 551, 800
France,
  French 941, 1034
Free 114, 278, 371, 534, 723, 821, 959, 1287
Freedom 101, 187, 209, 376, 377, 471, 545, 669, 685, 1157, 1283, 1285
Freedom of
  Speech 209
Friend 15, 159, 303, 328, 657, 730, 780, 797, 949, 1334, 1480, 1485, 1496, 1501, 1503
Fussbudget 8
Games 347
Gate 359, 360
Gender 1484
Generation 85, 216, 374, 689, 755, 916, 1165, 1166, 1216, 1410, 1422, 1466, 1468, 1472

Genius	376, 377, 1474		541, 544, 783,
German	1414, 1427		1045, 1211, 1424
Giant	255	Habit	225, 689, 690,
Gift (good)	130, 131, 392,		716, 1460, 1495,
	980, 981, 983,		1500
	1143, 1383, 1487	Handbook	361, 1427
Goal (life's)	188, 576, 722,	Hardship	751-753, 833
	732, 888, 1007,	Harlot	946
	1079, 1488, 1498	Harvest	1407
God is love	31, 375, 479, 481,	Healing	555
	489, 612, 723,	Health,	
	1487	Healthy	100, 813, 860,
God's name	36, 44, 364, 697		1465, 1489
God's will	16, 44, 1502	Heaven	8, 11, 23, 29, 63,
God's word	386, 779, 1108 -		76, 155, 183, 229,
	1110, 1112, 1115-		565, 657, 747,
	1117,1120, 1127		749, 778, 799,
God's wrath	17		804, 1091, 1146,
Gold	1436		1147, 1405, 1467,
Golden mean			1472
(the)	334	Heavenly	276, 303, 814,
Gospel	204, 300, 424,		840, 1173
	566, 616, 654,	Hegel	647, 896, 1067,
	913, 1135		1068, 1070, 1103,
Gossip	1203, 1417		1256, 1414, 1419
Grace	16, 17, 97, 314,	Heiberg	1449
	350, 664, 912,	Heine	1138
	1498	Hell	501
Grateful	130, 143, 225	Heresy	343
Gravestone	502	Hero	292, 518, 873,
Greatness	62, 110		885, 886, 1370
Greek	317, 430, 723,	Heterogeneity	97, 327, 344
	1142	Hide, Hidden	65, 68, 218, 488,
Grief	486		541, 781, 788,
Grocers	1067, 1143		1205
Guilt, Guilty	21, 305, 402,	Hiding place	81, 131, 241, 492,
	431, 432, 439,		659
	479, 481, 532,		
	535, 537, 538,		

History,
  Historical 293, 361, 792,
    823, 864, 893,
    1062, 1063
Holy 13, 23, 47, 536,
    857
Holy
  Scripture 266, 845
Holy Spirit 925, 1486
Home 159, 259, 306,
    352, 383, 453,
    647, 1151, 1365,
    1445, 1481, 1491,
    1498
Homeless 81
Homesick-
    ness 897
Homogeneous 144, 274, 327,
    1097, 1131
Honest,
  Honesty 183, 251, 348,
    351, 362, 541,
    542, 799, 803,
    1040, 1487
Honor 479, 707, 887,
    967, 1175, 1191,
    1329, 1353, 1440,
    1481, 1488, 1500
Honorary
  Christians 330, 1490
Honorary
  Doctors 330
Honor
 (this world's) 179, 186, 243,
    1098, 1144, 1236
House,
  Household 839, 1365, 1490
House
    (God's) 436, 437, 773,
    796, 1477

House
 (of the Lord) 252, 253
Human
Improvement 22
Hypocrite 566, 848, 1192,
    1232
Hypothesis 1060
Idea 9, 104, 107, 211,
    212, 213, 227,
    378, 448, 864,
    1085, 1188, 1234,
    1346, 1477, 1488,
    1492
Ideal 227, 237, 388,
    454, 584, 997,
    1011, 1132, 1133
Idol, Idolize 36, 1440, 1477
Illusion 171, 173, 174,
    224, 358, 400,
    607, 1001, 1230,
    1234, 1493
Image 1326. 1467, 1477
Image of God 5, 53
Imagination 309, 338, 588,
    942, 1022, 1312,
    1496, 1498
Imitation
  (of Christ) 95, 96, 275, 362,
    366, 392, 485,
    688, 1133, 1383
Immediacy 562, 802, 1153
Immediate(ly) 293, 465, 491,
    527, 530, 741,
    1167, 1200, 1381,
    1422, 1487
Immoral 890
Immortal (ity) 166, 1053-1055,
    1308
Impatience 469, 633

Impenitence 1207
Impiety 1353
Impossible 82, 240, 471, 661,
792, 1059, 1421
Impoverished 41, 1091
Imprison 72, 240
Improbable 399
Incarnation 67, 69, 84, 88
Incognito 92
Independence 112, 113, 1328
Indifference 274, 321, 332,
359, 381, 500,
698, 973, 1125,
1178, 1280, 1486
Individual
(ethical) 880, 881
Inferiors 1066
Infinite 23, 24, 26, 45, 84,
192, 205, 271,
487, 493, 516,
576, 580, 610,
642, 643, 662,
678, 713, 762,
789, 790, 797,
799, 965, 983,
1037, 1059, 1061,
1178, 1229, 1337,
1339, 1409
Innocence,
Innocent 121, 1027, 1056,
1342, 1424, 1487
Insignificant 570, 713, 768,
983, 1018, 1460
Institution 1079, 1156
Instruction 22, 111
Intellectual 518, 554, 1034,
1487
Intelligence 1127
Intoxication 1185

Inwardness 181, 213, 466,
588, 714, 717,
921, 930, 941,
968, 1155
Jew, Jewish 317, 723, 1369
Jinni 1463
Job 460, 684, 1412
Journey 1279, 1302, 1416,
1478
Joy 39, 98, 458, 481,
493, 705, 806,
834, 856, 903,
991, 1351, 1397,
1471
Judas kiss 241
Judge 80, 179, 224, 989,
990, 1181, 1268,
1412, 1488
Judgment 80, 179, 196, 197,
340, 989, 990,
1054, 1055
Juliet 1347
Justice 154, 295, 990
King 33, 74, 675, 727,
1435, 1479, 1493,
1494, 1500
Kingdom 169, 386, 1173,
1187, 1197, 1330,
1341, 1349, 1409,
1464
Knight 292, 1075
Know oneself 188
Laughter 168, 228, 1354,
1459, 1486, 1496
Lazy 225, 309
Leap (the) 123, 674, 678,
1266, 1505
Lemonade 390

Leniency 300, 418, 990
Lessing, G.E. 1241, 1246
Leveling 190, 193, 217, 1322
Life-view 276, 278, 918, 927, 928
Lie, Liar 254, 375, 1177, 1234
Lowly, Lowli-
ness 607, 728, 729, 1191, 1327
Luck 644
Luther 349, 665
Madness 828, 1314
Magister 169, 1262
Malpractice 346
Market
(place) 225, 1473
Martensen
(Bishop) 347
Martyr,
Martyrdom 168, 529, 1156
Masquerade 347
Maxim 604
Medal (s) 179, 1329
Medical,
Medicine 139, 371, 1441
Mediocrity 236, 388, 454, 1132, 1168
Meekness 811, 812
Memorize
(the Bible) 1021
Mene mene 277
Merchant 354, 1493
Microscope 1399, 1461
Middle Ages 335, 1152
Midnight 239, 795
Millions 95, 353, 368, 388, 607, 1216, 1390, 1422

Mirror 1030, 1109, 1110, 1113, 1114, 1326
Misfortune 465, 628, 633, 642, 1487
Missionary 339
Misunder-
stand (ing) 267, 430, 681, 740, 826, 1071
Misunder-
stood 817, 1419
Mock(ery) 95, 105, 141, 330, 821, 1287, 1313, 1488
Monastery 1098, 1152
Monasticism 1097
Money 330, 389, 945, 980, 1172, 1188, 1213, 1426, 1433, 1446, 1448, 1452, 1491, 1496, 1501, 1503
Mood 711, 872, 941, 953, 1131, 1134, 1309
Moon 523
Moral 554, 885, 1496
Moses 3
Mouth 928, 1097, 1206
Mynster
(Bishop) 317, 335, 342, 343, 345, 346, 393, 395
Mystery 62, 776
Mysticism 1404
Name
(Christian) 330, 356, 368, 378, 381, 1235
Name (God's) 36, 44, 336, 364, 697

Index

Name
  (the only) 747
Napoleon 1472
Natural 109, 137, 184, 208, 259, 428, 453, 472, 527, 718, 740, 1238, 1247, 1266, 1461, 1498
Nature 62, 111, 356, 376, 445, 458, 723, 1192, 1300, 1487
Neighbor 15, 235, 265, 266, 720
Neutral 276, 1360
New Testament 345, 348, 349, 352, 357, 360, 361, 364, 374, 390, 1121, 1122, 1375
Nice (ness) 28, 754
Niger River 1309
Nothing too much 604
Numbers 198, 222, 1156, 1496
Oath 370
Obesity (carnal) 331
Objectivity 274, 294, 907, 967, 1119, 1120, 1261, 1305
Ocean 1174, 1466, 1467
Offense 82, 83, 317, 455, 718, 723, 1063, 1360
Official (officialdom) 24, 352, 362, 390, 556, 1494

Omnipotence 61, 112, 113, 1496
Omnipresent 670
Omniscience 195, 547
Opinion 215, 242, 251, 356, 372, 382, 629, 805, 897, 1148, 1185, 1189, 1202, 1215, 1216, 1457
Opposite 35, 83, 128, 231, 497, 559, 561, 616, 648, 701, 722, 774, 1122, 1165, 1190, 1210
Ordinary 97, 102, 103, 376, 796, 1099, 1134
Orthodox 398
Pagan, Paganism 14, 15, 46, 67, 122, 320, 321, 325, 330, 339, 358, 428, 479, 642, 644, 711, 714, 810, 858, 859, 995, 1113, 1258, 1311
Pantheism 234, 825
Paradox 83, 290, 291, 598, 920, 1061, 1063
Paralogism 210, 517, 918
Parents 315, 400, 1017, 1031
Particular (the) 97, 124, 192, 241, 315, 361, 444, 540, 561, 795, 826, 864, 991, 1015, 1185, 1434

Party
  (celebration) 1031
Party (group) 238, 673, 961
Pathos 10, 228
Paul 1124
Peace 208, 301, 424,
  616, 796, 834
Peasant 1327, 1491
Peking 1478
Pelagianism 430
Penitence,
  Penitent 76, 551, 816,
  300, 874, 1044
Perdition 300, 874, 1044
  1051, 1226
Perfection 18, 38, 57, 131,
  265, 310, 386,
  391, 624, 683,
  863, 986, 1155,
  1409
Persecution 306, 318, 484,
  660, 1372
Peter 684, 688
Petitio Pricipii 1211
Pharisee 560, 566, 1077,
  1232
Philistine 494
Philosopher 645, 701, 807,
  828, 871, 1077
Philosophy 101, 646-648,
  838, 896, 1032,
  1077, 1256, 1278,
  1289, 1414
Physician 372, 926, 1093,
  1413, 1431, 1441,
  1473, 1489
Piety 9, 914, 1026,
  1027, 1369
Pilate 1057
Play 343, 365, 375,
  394, 436, 810,

  1023, 1030, 1193,
  1356, 1481, 1494,
  1505, 1506
Policeman 159, 439, 897,
  1274, 1422
Political 229, 1156
Politics 231, 429, 1155
Possess 99, 179, 262, 283,
  357, 729, 851,
  857, 867, 1145,
  1188, 1464, 1470,
  1503
Possibility 347, 494, 641,
  659, 727, 819,
  1031, 1160, 1285,
  1422
Poverty 667, 846, 856,
  857, 1485, 1504
Praise 38, 39, 200, 243,
  986, 1204, 1454,
  1480, 1503
Pray 153, 551, 567,
  635, 815, 841,
  843, 844, 1477,
  1504
Prayer 364, 564, 565,
  621, 1210, 1464
Preach 345, 346, 795,
  937, 1085, 1099,
  1104, 1157, 1300,
  1498
Preacher 346, 549, 550,
  734
Press (the) 1162, 1163, 1205-
  1207, 1209, 1211,
  1216, 1217
Presumption 19, 54-56, 69,
  330, 354, 368,
  665, 681, 813,
  1233, 1246, 1342

Price	45, 355, 469, 647, 966, 1197, 1217, 1270, 1371, 1414, 1448, 1495, 1496	Pure	111, 192, 402, 481, 1071, 1421, 1487
Pride	430, 812, 997, 1201, 1464, 1487	Purpose	106, 278, 646, 759
Prince	1455, 1464, 1470	Pythagorean	1218
Private	535, 886, 1251, 1494	Quack	926
		Quarreling	744
		Queen	1459
Probable	67. 332, 357, 398, 399, 696, 698, 746, 1427, 1481	Questions	72, 180, 201, 241, 299, 682, 845, 1031, 1131, 1241, 1444, 1459, 1487
Professional	1096		
Profligacy	141	Reading	158, 159, 162, 361, 1108, 1110, 1115, 1116, 1210, 1461
Progress	30, 153, 419		
Proof	654		
Prophet	1118, 1119, 1504		
Prosperity	279, 280, 282, 1002	Reconcilia-tion	555, 878
Prostitutes	1480	Recognition	163, 1311
Protect, Protection	44, 383, 1095, 1372, 1487	Redeem, Redeemer	75, 815, 932, 1316, 1482
Protest	1200, 1201	Reflection	135, 184, 191, 273, 466, 467, 583, 814, 961, 965, 1160, 1281, 1321
Prototype	53, 73, 93, 97, 737, 759, 765, 1133, 1232, 1468		
Proud	14, 41, 568, 569, 724, 1409, 1493, 1495, 1500	Regret	12, 543, 544, 1046
Proverb	1397, 1442	Reitzel's (bookstore)	159
Providence	278, 1230		
Pseudonymity	165	Relationship	14, 46, 270, 276, 301, 302, 604, 614, 678, 836, 886, 974
Public	157-159, 162, 167, 226, 382, 425, 1136, 1162-1165, 1189, 1202, 1236, 1494		
		Relationship to God	3, 46, 54, 180, 349, 447, 468, 475, 520, 681
Publicity	1158		

Religion 284, 316, 381, 429, 447, 530, 673, 685, 916, 1388

Remember 295, 560, 563, 815, 1033, 1108, 1362, 1473, 1482

Remind 806, 815, 1142, 1364, 1414

Renounce 136, 221, 1148
Renunciation 306, 335, 342, 391, 530, 1079, 1148

Repent 12, 302, 346, 443, 1482

Resolution
(the) 4, 596, 666, 668, 1002, 1003, 1160, 1281

Responsi-
bility 98, 179, 220, 235, 392, 683, 1009, 1141, 1165, 1207, 1224, 1383, 1443

Responsible 149, 660, 881, 1487

Rest 66, 551, 1369

Restless 159, 306, 993, 1092

Revealed
(truth) 68, 270, 617, 1220

Revelation 441, 499, 1404

Revolution 628, 706, 1034, 1161

Rich 667, 736, 1188, 1248, 1485, 1495

Righteous 48, 207, 260, 1055, 1504

Righteousness 535, 538, 1173, 1433

Risk 179, 228, 230, 294

Road (the) 249, 424, 450, 553, 745-747, 749-753, 1434, 1469, 1491

Road
(crossroad) 683

Robes (long) 1096

Rule, Ruler 105, 423, 426, 810, 1141, 1327, 1409

Rule
(standard) 743, 1200, 1206, 1417

Rumor 1199

Sacred 902, 1428

Sacrifice 31, 45, 306, 323, 330, 397, 420, 656, 682, 688, 888, 899, 976, 991, 1056, 1451

Sacrificed
One 31

Saints 32

Saint-
Simonist 1034

Sale, For Sale 354, 945, 1171, 1200

Saloonkeeper 1496

Salt 1451

Salvation 300, 308, 387, 708, 814, 1102, 1219

Samaritan 424

Save, Saved 314, 501, 528, 635, 655, 658, 660, 664, 665, 840, 1079, 1268, 1460

Savior 96, 240, 357, 392,
474, 560, 815,
932, 1383
Scandal 145
Scholar 191, 274, 621,
793, 1394, 1487
School 475-478, 944,
1033, 1258
Schoolmaster 1350
Science 124, 274, 476,
1398, 1461
Scribes 560
Scripture 266, 428, 468,
845
Secret 65, 131, 135, 251,
262, 334, 492,
673, 708, 795,
1035, 1208, 1400
Secular 274, 1131, 1134,
1178, 1181, 1235
Seducer 197, 939, 942, 999,
1219
Seduction 943, 1012
Seers of Egypt 3
Self 205, 206, 428,
493, 561, 618,
694, 801, 802,
1355, 1357
Self-annihila-
tion 520
Self-concern 301, 723, 1487
Self-contra-
diction 133, 1127
Self-control 1430
Self-deception 259, 453, 1222,
1224, 1229
Self-denial 235, 251, 266,
306, 326, 530,
1079
Self-esteem 1230

Self-evident 324
Self-giving 954
Self-know-
ledge 1113
Self-loss 801
Self-love 15, 971, 1363,
1387
Self-torment 630
Self-will 128, 409, 428,
522, 649
Selfish 18, 115, 124, 127,
424, 523, 525,
526, 562, 948
Sensuous 115, 948, 1482
Sentimental 723
Separation 213, 930, 1055
Sermon 334, 363, 386,
1082, 1488, 1498
Sexual 937
Shakespeare 578
Shallow (s) 184, 903, 1505
Sheep 848
Shop, Shop-
keeper 352, 1437, 1461
Sick 139, 140, 259,
453, 813, 926,
1201, 1441, 1489
Sickbed 795, 1441
Sickly-sweet 723
Sign, Signs 3, 475, 603, 1502
Significance 211, 262, 477,
570, 713, 1206,
1459, 1484
Silence 1218, 1252, 1365,
1367
Simple 7, 18, 185, 336,
455, 701, 895,
1154, 1224, 1256,
1339
Singer (a) 1312

Skeptic,
   Skepticism 828, 1074
Sober 741, 783, 1185
Socrates 440, 518, 1033,
   1038, 1268, 1409,
   1424, 1461, 1474
Socratic 651, 1216
Soldier 365, 388, 1453,
   1470
Son of man 353
Sophist,
   Sophistical 690, 933, 1457,
   1461
Sorrow 51, 456, 458, 493,
   552, 839, 870,
   924
Soul 9, 67, 129, 308,
   433, 551, 645,
   655, 670, 709,
   1144, 1225, 1246,
   1273, 1286, 1339,
   1487, 1506
Sparrow 26
Speech 209, 775, 1095,
   1220, 1288
Spiritless 463, 494, 496,
   500, 579
Spiritual 79, 223, 231, 259,
   277, 311, 371,
   411, 412, 424,
   453, 463, 524,
   724, 752, 771,
   1142, 1284, 1391,
   1396, 1411, 1437,
   1473
Spring (season) 1405, 1483
Spring (water) 584, 1497
Stars 17, 76, 1466

State
(the political) 336, 353, 367,
   897, 1142, 1209,
   1372
State
(condition) 259, 371, 444, 453,
   524, 675, 1185,
   1211, 1286, 1491
Stoicism 206, 276, 345
Struggle 410, 413, 416,
   417, 464, 568,
   1407
Subjective 793, 907, 1118
Success 155, 274, 1190
Suicide 59, 676
Sun 1327
Sunday 363, 1092, 1459,
   1498
Swine,
   Swineherd 817
Syrupy sweets 375
Talleyrand 1220, 1250
Tantalus 1155
Task (the) 12, 42, 46, 73,
   185, 277, 283,
   480, 481, 568,
   570, 606, 645,
   717, 793, 883,
   892, 1041, 1192,
   1489
Tax Collector 1232
Teacher 22, 87, 179, 240,
   303, 651, 746,
   1096, 1352, 1392,
   1505
Telos 133, 602, 604,
   606, 824, 885
Temporal 8, 149, 155, 266,
   282, 423, 482,
   545, 632, 830,

949, 1047-1049, 1051, 1059, 1065, 1146, 1431, 1436, 1482

Temptation 446, 615, 847, 1319

Test 415, 975, 985

Theater 385, 619, 865, 1445, 1462

Theological 1079

Thief 145, 179, 840, 1433

Third Party 673, 961

Throne 329, 649, 1504

Thunder 1460

Today 375, 629, 630, 634, 635, 638, 1064, 1082, 1111, 1157, 1210, 1432

Tomorrow 427, 507, 629, 636, 638, 852, 1157, 1210, 1432

Tragic 292, 518, 872, 885, 886, 1107, 1140

Traitor 794

Transform 530, 601, 1153, 1192, 1193, 1206, 1415

Transmigration 67

Travel 361, 424, 756, 1421, 1446, 1469, 1478

Treason 450, 906, 751

Trick 86, 751, 980, 1458

Trinity 1035

Troops 1439, 1472

Truth-
Witness 95, 96, 343, 344, 346, 1100

Umpire 1465

Uncertain 688, 1049

Unfaithful 302, 855, 1501

Uncle 6

Unconditional 39, 149, 234, 265, 329, 355, 378, 379, 397, 522, 528, 572, 587, 609, 616, 619, 753, 779, 913, 947, 980, 1046, 1092

Unfaithful 302, 855, 1501

Ungrateful 225

Unhappy 502, 879, 1147, 1233

Unhealthy 331

Union 1008, 1014, 1147

Universal 103, 290-292, 884, 1136, 1258, 1462

University degree 169

Unmask 239

Untruth 198, 245, 247, 262, 263, 266, 269, 306, 761, 926, 1183, 1212, 1227, 1236, 1367, 1477

Unworthiness 161

Upbuilding 78, 252, 813, 1225

Vain 199, 527, 576, 628, 746

Valid, Validity 604, 882, 995, 1136, 1142
Vanity 538, 569
Venture, Venturing 604, 654, 691, 696, 697, 702
Venus 548
Victorious 60, 89, 234, 327, 1407, 1408
Victory 14, 60, 78, 254, 398, 416, 464, 724, 725, 812, 874, 1151, 1395
Violence 167, 213, 1464
Virtue 128, 288, 596, 667, 750, 885, 1198, 1409
Vogue (in) 178
Waders 903
Wardrobe 1449
Water (Baptism) 373
Water (drinking) 584, 903, 1200, 1410, 1425, 1463, 1497, 1505
Wealth 179, 1426, 1474
Weary 76, 1119, 1272
Weed 307
Whisper 1320, 1479
Wine 390, 1410, 1463
Wisdom 86, 143, 326, 567, 604, 769, 1073, 1208, 1457, 1464
Witness 95, 96, 117, 306, 343, 344, 346, 375, 650, 663, 923, 1083, 1089, 1100, 1106, 1226
Witticism 14, 937, 1206

Wonder 34, 35, 41, 353, 501, 570, 670, 1001, 1018, 1020, 1278, 1289, 1486
Wonderful 32, 563, 864, 1013
Worldly 114, 133, 179, 194, 266, 276, 538, 604, 631, 721, 727, 729, 809, 1148, 1196, 1488
World-view 918, 1194
Worship 95, 364, 864, 1246, 1477, 1488, 1498, 1501
Wound 462, 526, 549, 1092, 1431, 1487
Wrath (God's) 17
Wretchedness 20, 21, 114, 524, 574, 667, 1091, 1487
Xanthippe 1033, 1038, 1424
Xenophon 1038
Years ago 95, 1056, 1063, 1064, 1459
Youth 250, 806, 878, 1044, 1067, 1079, 1234
Zeal, Zealous 45, 1223, 1481
Zealot 580
Zeno 828

To order additional copies of

Kierkegaard
the Christian

Have your credit card ready and call

Toll free: (877) 421-READ (7323)

or send $17.00* each plus $5.95 S&H** to

WinePress Publishing
PO Box 428
Enumclaw, WA 98022

or order online at: www.winepresspub.com

*Washington residents, add 8.4% sales tax
**add $1.50 S&H for each additional book ordered